Fully Persuaded Faith

MARILYNN JAMES

Cover design by Gayle Jenkins-Diaz

Fully Persuaded Faith

ISBN 0-88144-320-4

Printed by
Thorncrown Publishing
A Division of Yorkshire Publishing Group
7707 East 111th Street South, Suite 104
Tulsa, Oklahoma 74133
www.yorkshirepublishing.com

DEDICATION

Fully Persuaded Faith is dedicated to Darnell, Dwight and Melissa James. Their humor and perspectives have been spring boards for this book. Appreciation goes to Melissa for her first draft of the book cover; Dwight finalized my thoughts regarding the cover, so that I could provide the second draft to the publisher. Sister Presita May gave her time and expertise to depict the cover also.

Next, I wish to **personally thank** Sister Freda Robinson and her mother, Sister Lorraine Gibbs, for their ongoing, consistent prayers to spearhead this project from conception to completion, including recommending an artist to finalize the book cover!!

Lastly, my heartfelt thanks go to both my editors, Renee McCline and Modupe Oladeinde for the hours they spent adding *comments and encouragement* to this project as it progressed toward completion! Renee recommended chapter ten, since her family was positively impacted during many times of crisis with answered prayer when we prayed. Modupe gained a new outlook about the type of faith we all should embrace as she edited the book. Per Modupe, we should only approach God with fully persuaded faith.

INTRODUCTION

The purpose of <u>**"Fully Persuaded Faith"**</u> is to encourage Christians to continue to pray fervently according to James 5:15 for each situation, challenge, attack, undesired circumstance and stage of one's life, since "the effectual fervent prayer of a righteous man avails much". Often, prayer is used as a <u>**last**</u> resort, when in fact; prayer should be used as the first line of defense against the devil's tactics each time a situation surfaces.

The Lord advised two of us to "touch and agree on any request", so that He could perform the request for the petitioners, according to Matthew 18:19:

"Again I say unto you, that if two of you shall agree on earth as touching any thing that they shall ask, it shall be done for them of my Father which is in heaven".

The pages of <u>**"Fully Persuaded Faith"**</u> will re-cap God's <u>great faithfulness</u> in our everyday lives over the past decade or so. The examples are ones that other families have faced or will face. These examples can indeed serve as a support to anyone in a storm.

Since we know that God is the same, yesterday, today and forever (Hebrews 13:8), our experiences are written to give the reader hope. <u>**GOD NEVER CHANGES.**</u> Decades and technology do change, yet God's prevailing glory remains the same. His on-time deliverance is forever the same. Hence, <u>**"Fully Persuaded Faith"**</u> will document His glory in <u>this generation!</u>

The author, Marilynn James, wants each reader to have a brief personal, spiritual and professional synopsis about the specific demographics regarding the writer.

Personal History

The writer is the second child of five and is married with two (2) grown children. The oldest sibling, Linda, is married and has two (2) grown sons. Wayne is the third sibling; he is married with two (2) grown sons. Korveeta is the fourth child and is not married. Cornelius is the youngest; he has two (2) children. He has had multiple sclerosis at varying stages over the past ten (10) years.

The writer began to pray diligently for God's partner upon the horizon around 18 years old. The writer wrote out specifics about this **unknown** man: he needed to be 5'11, a dedicated Christian, friendly and a person who enjoyed giving his time, expertise or money when needed. God sent such a man through Marilynn's co-worker and the unknown man's then older brother, these gentlemen orchestrated this match! Marilynn (Mahone) James and Darnell James dated for approximately one and half years prior to their union on May 25, 1985.

When the family expanded, Dwight (1987) and Melissa (1989) were born. The children provided many reasons to pray as they grew. Dwight was a fantastic boy who climbed on or flipped over everything. We held our breath when he fell after climbing or jumping unexpectedly. Melissa's asthma diagnosis kept us seeking God for rhythmical breathing miracles. As they grew, we learned that God was preparing us for greater prayer combat through our children's situations. Later, these same prayer requests would transfer to others' concerns for their children.

Spiritual History

As a young Christian, the writer attended a church with primarily middle aged and retired Christians. This made a great impact on the writer as faith was expressed often and readily. This genre of churchgoers felt that faith and prayer cured everything immediately.

Education was not emphasized in that church, [since education was considered a "worldly encounter"]. However, the writer asked God to avert any denouncement of God as the writer completed college, since students may not find value in church activities during early adult years.

During high school and college, the writer taught Sunday School, directed the choir, led Praise and Worship services as well as made fast friends with a ninety (90+) year old deacon. This friendship aided the writer in actively seeking God for life's answers when problems surfaced, since the deacon had utilized God's power for over forty (40) years.

God gave the writer an ability to formulate prayer requests as situations are described. Through the years, many individuals have appreciated this gift — when no prayer came immediately to their own minds.

Concurrently with prayer and right living, this writer has taught various seminars in various churches regarding faith, leadership, planning, wellness and family management, by God's help.

Pastor William (Bill) Winston actively demonstrates faith at Living Word Christian Center, the writer's home church for almost seven years. Pastor Winston invites many encouraging faith leaders to visit Living Word Christian Center in Forest Park, IL to perpetuate faith in members. These ministers strengthened faith through their teachings and have served as models to finish this work. Jerry Savelle proclaimed in 2005 that "God is the God of the **<u>break-through</u>**. This work needed a break-through for completion. Next, Pastor Paula White declared during her 2007 visit that "the church has entered a time to **<u>be celebrated, not tolerated</u>**". Hence, the church needed to ask God to send people that needed our particular style of ministry". Subsequently, this author resumed praying diligently after Pastor White's visit to complete this work.

At the present time, the writer volunteers in the Adult Education Ministry (AEM) at Living Word Christian Center (LWCC) in Spanish instruction as a means to advance the kingdom for those who do or will do mission work in Spanish-speaking communities or countries.

Professional History

The writer completed bachelors degrees in Nursing and in Spanish. Later, the writer finished a master's degree in nursing. These talents have been used to give God glory as the writer worked in hospitals, industry and church when individuals needed guidance regarding medical conditions or prayer for those same conditions. Many prayer assignments were encountered in the nursing profession.

As a point of sharing with the community-at-large, the writer has served as an adjunct faculty member at University of Illinois, St. Xavier and Aurora University Nursing Schools and presented seminars at many national occupational health nursing conferences.

Since the author has experienced many challenges as life progressed, [it seemed befitting to share with the readers] the circumstances described in this book document that God's power remains the same in a modern world that prefers to exclude His wisdom and righteousness from daily living.

Hebrew 13:8 reminds us that God is the same, yesterday, today and forever. The following pages will highlight God's **great** faithfulness.

ACKNOWLEDGMENTS

I acknowledge God for His "tender fingers of mercy" as He has strategically placed a mighty army of prayer warriors in our lives. In the late 1980's, we prayed for "good friends", especially "good couple friends". I wondered how God would connect others to us. He did so with two church moves and an out-of-state prayer retreat that Darnell attended since He knew our future challenges. These connections occurred over a 10 year span.

I honor my deceased parents, Gordon and Effie Mahone, as pastors of the Apostolic Faith Church in Evanston, Illinois, for their dedication to spiritual things during my teens and young adult life.

I want to express gratitude for my husband, Darnell, who has been steadfast in prayer with me in each stage of our lives. I thank Dwight and Melissa, our young adults, for their willingness to bring school, basketball and poetry club issues home with requests for prayer. Without these issues, I would not have sought the depths of prayer that I now know!

Special thanks to Evangelist Shirley Davis for her unrelenting prayers and agreement since 1990. She is a true friend, who has modeled effective prayer in her monthly prayer meetings since 1993 and has supported us in all phases of our family's development.

Sister Freda Robinson and her mom, Sister Lorraine Gibbs, have prayed for this book fervently for more than twelve years. Both have encouraged us countless times from New York as we faced difficult family circumstances.

I want to especially thank God for Sister Toni Horras, Sister Kathryn Kircher, Sister Joy Hudson and Sister Marilyn Foster for their consistent prayers with me for our children and families as our children grew in the spirit and admonition of the Lord from 1996-2007. They have been exceptional role models as wives, mothers and school activists.

Deacon Lamont and Evangelist Florence Johnson, Sister Gloria Williams, Pastor Al and Evangelist Ever Houston and Sister Tanya Briggs were given to us as "true yoke fellow friends", according to Philippians 4:3. We met all of them while we attended Truth and Deliverance Church in Chicago, IL. All are ready "prayer warriors" morning, noon or night plus weekends!

Sister Tiffany Martin-Baker and her family, Tamika and Teresse Martin, Judy and Barbara Gould along with Corey Lewis have been staunch and intuitive prayer warriors. They are easily accessible by email or text messaging and also are friends through Truth and Deliverance Church.

Sister Loretta Wilson and Sister Joyce Williams have been available prayer warriors at work. Both have believed for impossible things with us. They never tire of trusting God's power **now**.

Pastor Rick and Sister Betsy Bullis taught us the power of "not seeing, yet believing" when Dwight was struck by a taxi in May 2001. They prayed fervently for Dwight's deliverance from any injury that day.

Sister Evelyn Watt, now 96, has walked through life with us in prayer for more than 40 years. She trusts God and lets it be known.

Pastor Johnny and Mrs. Beatrice Lay have shown hospitality and concern for us during our visits to California. During significant family trials, Pastor Johnny Lay has been a marvelous example of a Shepherd supporting the Sheep of God during crises with multiple, ongoing prayers and pertinent scriptures.

Deacon Calvin and Evangelist Virginia Brown joined our lives through a retreat event in Whitewater, Wisconsin. This connection taught me to seek God diligently for who the contacts in our lives should be.

Brother Greg and Sister Sheryl Thomas have become manifestations of God's glory as we have prayed for their faith to increase over the last eleven years. Now, we have fervent prayer warriors. What I appreciate most about Sister Sheryl is her forthright approach with Melissa, our daughter. These interactions have had an immeasurable effect in Melissa's life.

Special mention goes to Toni and Elisabeth Dlutowski, who acted as surrogate grandparents as Dwight and Melissa grew and Christine Provost, Dwight's godmother, who has staunchly supported the children during every stage of their lives! Brother John and Evangelist Gwen Golliday, Melissa's godparents, Uncle Walter and Aunt Lillie Hopkins, Aunt Geraldine James have under girded us with prayer and hand-on interventions when needed.

Lastly, Renee McCline is a friend that sticks closer than any brother or sister could ever hope to do. During family trials, she swings by to lend a hand as often as needed!

All have offered discernment, encouragement, experience, strong prayers and wisdom continually for many years. They have been attuned to the Spirit of God and obeyed when God gave them a message for our family.

To God be the glory!

Scripture Reference

Romans 4:20-21 KJV

"Abraham staggered not at the promise of God through unbelief;
but was strong in faith, giving glory to God;
And being <u>fully persuaded</u> that
what God had promised, He
was able to perform.

FOREWORD

This book is intended to bolster the faith of those who are challenged with work, family, trials, illness, accidents, injuries, school, job loss and life's storms, etc.

Secondly, this book is to glorify God for His mercy, truth and great faithfulness to my family and me. I realize that God's hand of protection and wisdom has guided us through many highways in life.

Thirdly, I wish to encourage all of those thinking and contemplating writing their own story to do so, since this book has been forming in my mind and heart for eleven years. During 2005 when my father was sick and subsequently passed away, I continued to ponder the chapters for this project. This book was ultimately birthed during two great family trials in 2007:

1) My mom's tremendous fight for life as she battled cancer and;

2) My brother's five month hospitalization for progressive Multiple Sclerosis (aka MS). Write with God's help.

As you read, I have noted within these pages how God delivers. I did not always like how God delivered. Yet, I must report that God joined us faithfully in each fiery furnace like the three (3) Hebrew men (Daniel 3:3-30) and every lion's den like Daniel, (Daniel 6:7-23).

As a result of multiple prayer situations, I have added additional prayer points to each request when I pray now.

For example: I usually pray for newborns and their parents for God's direction and understanding. Now, the request must include future friends, acquaintances and teachers, since these parties play an important role in a child's growth and development. In light of the Columbine High School, Virginia Tech and recent NIU massacres, one must extend prayers of protection across the nation and the world.

Be blessed and joyful as we continue to serve the King of Kings!

TABLE OF CONTENTS

CHAPTER ONE

The Millennium: The Age of Technology

In the age of Blackberries, cell phones with cameras, iPods and pod casts, we are comfortable with the technological changes that the new millennium has afforded our lives. However, this fact was not the case as we ended the last century.

In 1997, my husband began to pray with me for wisdom for the Y2K initiative. At that time, all employees working with computers or linked to computer systems were gearing up for the "hypothetical" impending disaster as the year 2000 approached. Everyone felt that computers needed to be set for the new millennium.

My husband asked God for enlightenment for his Systems Department at his place of employment. He began inquiring with his boss, other systems managers and his co-workers about plans for the upcoming cycle in 2000.

He advised me that we needed to pray fervently to access God's ingenuity for this "**major project.**" As we all know, when we approach any out of the ordinary situation, we wonder in the back of our minds, "how God will deliver?"

We may not say it, but the thoughts flood our minds and hearts when we least need them to do so. Human nature assists us here and the devil.

My husband kept advising the management team to consider the magnitude of the endeavor. Of course, some managers thought they could wait until the year 2000 was closer, before commencing on the project.

My husband's tasks were to: 1) get managers onboard regarding the need for a planned approach to the task and 2) get everyone rolling on the components necessary for success.

Christians may wish to reference Sanballat and Tobiah in Nehemiah 4:8 here:

"And conspired all of them together to come and to fight against Jerusalem, and to hinder it."

There is always someone that nay says or wants to hinder the technique that God drops in your mind and/or lays on your heart. However, we must persevere to accomplish God's work and purpose in our lives.

Prayer Jewels:

1) Pray for the whole team's success and salvation. You will observe the cohesiveness unfold.

2) "Behold, how good and how pleasant it is for brethren to dwell together in unity, Psalm 133:1.

Pray for the appropriate presentation of the idea(s) or projects and the informative critique to improve the plan.

This point proved very helpful for me as I prayed for my husband on this **major** project. Subsequently, I have prayed for him along the same lines as other projects followed. God calls us as wives and mothers to "be keepers at home", Titus 2:5. Yes, in these modern days many women work, however, we need to have a watchful eye about family issues and stay prayerful.

In retrospect, this prayer request over several years felt like it was a "cinch" to present to the Lord. **Of course, the answer is now known and the task is delivered.** I feel very comfortable <u>now</u> knowing that God showed my husband what to do on many sub-parts of this major assignment.

Let the truth be told, I spent several nights awake asking God to connect all of the dots for that big January 1, 2000 date. My husband had to stay up through the night, 12/31/99, until 4 a.m. to get everything connected. Calls starting pouring in on his pager around 9:30 p.m. from the processing centers relating the fact that processes did not recognize the new millennium's 2000 code.

In <u>every</u> instance, my husband and the team of programmers figured out what minute detail needed collaboration to get and keep all of the inter-twining points on target to process all of the systems for that night.

God was at work in their lives.

I had such a sense of relief when the first official run occurred on January 2, 2000. I knew that God had expanded my husband's programming skills (his coast) like Jabez' requested in I Chronicles 4:9-10. **Mission accomplished! Praise God!**

This prayer task strengthened my faith when things are unseen. Neither of us knew what issues would surface during the length of the project. We approached this prayer like the woman with the unjust judge. She knew that she needed to be avenged. The judge did not necessarily believe that he was required to attend to her request, however, her persistence paid off, St. Luke 18: 1-8:

¹And he spoke a parable unto them to this end, that men ought always to pray, and not to faint;

[2]Saying, There was in a city a judge, who feared not God, neither regarded man:

[3]And there was a widow in that city; and she came unto him, saying, Avenge me of mine adversary.

[4]And he would not for a while: but afterward he said within himself, though I fear not God, nor regard man;

[5]Yet because this widow troubles me, I will avenge her, lest by her continual coming she weary me.

[6]And the Lord said, Hear what the unjust judge said.

[7]And shall not God avenge his own elect, which cry day and night unto him, though he bear long with them?

[8]I tell you that he will avenge them speedily. Nevertheless when the Son of man cometh, shall he find faith on the earth?

The widow's request for justice and for closure occurred, but not without her involvement. To all Christians, be involved with your requests and needs. God does answer, Psalm 99:6!

Prayer Jewels Continued:

3) "Moses and Aaron among his priests, and Samuel among them that call upon his name; they called upon the LORD, and **he answered them**", Psalm 99:6.

4) "And **Jabez** was more honorable than his brethren: and his mother called his name **Jabez,** saying, because I bare him with sorrow,

   [10]And Jabez called on the God of Israel, saying, Oh that thou would bless me indeed, and enlarge my coast, and that thy hand might be with me, and that thou would keep me from evil, that it may not grieve me! And God granted him that which he requested", 1 Chronicles 4:9-10.

CHAPTER TWO

The Dream

I had a dream during the summer of 2002. The dream gave a panoramic view of many employees listening attentively about the specifics of their job loss in a "big auditorium" meeting place. My husband and I were perplexed with the content of the dream, since his bank did not have an extremely large meeting room as shown in the dream. We began to pray for employees to find other jobs and that there would not be any workplace violence.

Years passed. My husband and the other associates received an email advising them to go to a large local hotel for a meeting in November 2005. No further details were given.

We all know that there is no comparable feeling to being told that one will lose one's job. Yet, my husband heard this information in a very large meeting in November 2005 with other bank associates.

During the meeting, specifics regarding the future were scant. Employees only knew that their jobs were being off shored to India.

The initial reaction was shock. Then, anger surged. Then, disbelief crept in…computer programming jobs would actually be off-shored.

As mortal men, we may unknowingly put our trust in the security of a particular profession. We really need to have our trust firmly rooted in God. These situations demonstrate where our hope and trust lie.

My husband was called to another corporate meeting on February 28, 2006. He was given an "off payroll date" of July 31, 2006. He looked on the job posting boards for another job. None was available to match his skills at that time.

Since my husband had a financial planning gift and a minor in Accounting, he interviewed with Edward Jones twice. He did all of the door-to-door interviews required. Edwards Jones promised to place him in an office in our local village with a decreasing salary, since the job would ultimately become fully commission based.

My husband knew that he had a job; it was estimated that he would need 1.5 to 2 years to build an established customer base. Yet, he kept looking on the bank's job posting board.

In late June 2006, a job surfaced in the Community Reinvestment Department. We tweaked his resume for submission for the position. He did not hear anything from the company recruiters for weeks. Of course, the inner voice hints a doubtful thought, "maybe they won't call", as other programmers had experienced after submission for other positions.

As Christians, this was the time to be bold and declare that God's provision for us was just like His provision of a ram in the thicket for Abraham, Genesis 22:13-14. We simply held faith that God would do a divine connection. Meanwhile, my husband and three others on his team got an extension until October 31, 2006.

My husband did hear on July 28, 2006! Amazingly, his current boss was packing to leave for the July 31st, 2006 separation date. Company policy required that the manager to approve any interviewing. God left his old boss in place to confirm my husband's privilege of interviewing!

Prayer Jewel:

1) <u>Practice</u> believing God!

Approval given: interview, here we come. My husband spoke with the hiring manager on August 1, 2006; she was going on vacation. The Human Resource liaison was also going on vacation for a few days.

It is the hardest thing to wait for an answer. Time moves like a turtle in these instances. The spirit of anxiousness gets a bat out to whip us over our heads.

As a Proverbs 31 wife, I could feel my husband wanting an answer regarding the outcome of the interview. About a week and a half into the waiting period, I gave him a reading from the Couples' Bible about waiting. He read it and told me later that this information gave him great calm.

Finally, two weeks later the hiring manager returned. There was more delay regarding transferring intra-divisionally. He heard that discussions were in progress. Waiting is a virtue!

On August 29, 2006, my husband got the approval for the new job inside the bank in the Community Redevelopment Department! He began planning his departure from the IT-Computer Programming Department.

What my husband did not know was a hiring/transferring freeze loomed ahead on September, 1 2006. My husband contemplated starting the new job in October. He later learned that would possibly mean no raise in 2007. He nixed that choice.

Then, he thought about postponing his acceptance until September 8, 2006. That choice would have meant that the hiring freeze was in effect. God allowed Human Resources to advise him about the ramifications of all his thoughts regarding his transition. He accepted the job before September 1, 2006 and started a new career! Praise God!

The answer was delayed but not denied.

Prayer Jewels Continued:

2) Stay prayerful; don't allow the devil or other well-meaning people to get you distracted off of your desired prayer outcome.

3) Keep asking for God's divine wisdom and divine connections, so everything works to your favor.

4) Do not absorb other co-workers' words that "Human Resources will not call and interact with you". My husband affirmed to several co-workers throughout the waiting time that God would answer him and give him favor for the job. We always use St. Luke 2:52 to confirm that we have "favor with God and man".

5) [13] "Abraham looked up and there in a thicket he saw a ram [a] caught by its horns. He went over and took the ram and sacrificed it as a burnt offering instead of his son. [14] So Abraham called that place The Lord Will Provide. And to

6) This day it is said, "On the mountain of the LORD it will be provided," Genesis 22:13-14.

During his farewell luncheon with fifteen (15) IT (computer) co-workers, all expressed amazement that the transition even occurred and that the rapidity of the events. Many of them submitted resumes for posted jobs, yet they never got any calls from Human Resources.

His team marveled at his good fortune. My husband used the opportunity to witness about God's <u>great</u> faithfulness! We know that they will never forget!

During unsettled times, hearts are more open to the Word of truth. Use these opportunities to discuss the plan and purpose of God for all of our lives with unbelievers.

CHAPTER THREE

God's Sustaining Power — Psalms 55:22

I began driving my own car in October 1977 and I was very happy to buy my own car.

All passengers knew my procedure. Pray and ask God's blessings at the start of every trip. We asked that Jesus' blood cover and protect us. My mom said repeatedly," No one can say 'Jesus help us' faster than you when someone swerves in front of us".

It was a sunny evening on May 17, 2004 around 5:40 p.m. I was about five (5) minutes from home. I had been enjoying a gospel tape on the way home. As usual, I had started my trip with prayer. I had been on the expressway from Motorola in Schaumburg for over one hour. I was excited about getting home while there was still an opportunity to enjoy the evening; I thought about taking a walk. However, that plan was about to be interrupted.

Incident One — May 2004

A young woman approached the stop sign at Home Street. She was on the telephone and distracted. I felt that she would not stop. I moved more to the right on Jackson Street, since the young lady appeared to move through the stop sign at a speed greater than 25 m.p.h.

She rolled out into the thoroughfare and struck me. My car jumped the curve and missed a tree. I steered my car away from the house on the corner. It stopped on the grass. I stayed in my car. The young woman got out of her car and started cursing and stomping. I called the police and the insurance company. I was heartbroken that she struck my new car, which had only been cruising on Chicago land expressways four (4) months!

She continued to display her displeasure with the situation. I asked the Lord if He wanted me to get out of the car. He told me to stay inside and read the Scriptures — Isaiah 53 and Proverbs 3:8.

The police officer came to ask if I was okay and if I needed an ambulance. I told her, "no". Likewise, the young woman stated that she did not need that kind of assistance.

I was glad that I stayed in the car. The young woman told the officer that she ran into me in the thoroughfare. The officer issued her a ticket. Her car needed a tow truck. The young woman began stomping and shouting when she was given the ticket and saw that she could not drive her car.

I kept praying on the way home. It was a hard hit. That evening I felt the muscles stiffen in my neck, upper left shoulder and lower left side. I kept telling the devil that he was not victorious in my life. I got up to go to work the next day.

I saw that I was moving slowly. I kept stating the word of God. When I arrived to work, some co-workers laughed at my walking. This was very discouraging, yet I knew God as a great deliverer. I knew that "by His stripes I was already healed", according to Isaiah 53:5.

The pain was so excruciating that I found myself not thinking clearly. I called for an appointment with the local naprapath, Dr. Ted Rapacz, who I had seen previously when I broke a fall with my hands when I fell forwards at the curb in 2002. (A doctor of naprapathy has eight (8) years of training to learn how to adjust connective tissue [muscles and cartilage] through manipulation).

He saw me within two days. I got great relief. I kept speaking God's word; "I know that I'm healed by Jesus' stripes."

Sister Tanya Briggs called me a couple weeks later to inquire how I was after the incident. I told her that I needed her to agree again with me in prayer for pain relief. She responded, "I'll do better than that. I met a massage therapist that does house visits. I just scheduled you a visit with her. The Lord told me to assist you in pain relief right now. That's why I'm on the telephone. Please call her this evening and get your appointment set-up."

I rejoiced with her for her obedience! How faithful is the Lord in trials? Very faithful!

I called Maxzina Davis for an appointment. She came to my house and set-up in the family room. Sister Tanya paid for a one hour session. Sister Maxzina told me that she perceived that I had faith for deliverance. She gave me the other hour gratis. (Massage therapists in Illinois obtain seven (7) months of training in massage to increase blood flow through muscles and to promote relaxation).

I then realized why God had told me about Psalm 55:22 in March 2004. God wanted me to know that He had people that I did not know on dispatch to help me. **That was His sustaining power.** He also wanted me to know how **important** it is to obey "**right away**". Sister Tanya's obedience had been **crucial** to my ongoing mobility.

God reminded me often about Sister Tanya's obedience. She met me at a specific point of need. That is how others view...any Christian that arrives at a crucial point. I have ___not___ forgotten this lesson.

I was so glad that I was improved. I told the naprapath in late October 2004 that I did not need weekly visits anymore. I was healed and able to navigate with grace. He released me and we both rejoiced!

Incident Two

So, I followed the same prayer procedure as I started driving home on November 1, 2004. It was a rainy, cold night. The traffic was at a stand-still on all expressways according to the radio reports. I decided to take the streets home, so that the trip would be one hour and a half versus two hours.

As I proceeded south on Algonquin Road, I heard a crunch sound behind me. It was the sound of a 2000 Honda striking against my right rear bumper. The driver was very apologetic. He said that he knew he needed to buy new tires, since he was experiencing a lot of sliding without rainy conditions. I kept thinking, "why didn't he get new tires before this event?"

We waited for the police. I began to pray against the spasm feelings that were trying to creep in my lower back and upper left neck. These spasms were grabbing my attention rapidly. I kept rebuking the feelings of pain. I took a muscle relaxant that I had with me from the May 2004 incident. I continued to state out loud, "there is health to my navel and marrow to my bones as written in Proverbs 3:8 plus "he was wounded for my transgressions and by his stripes I am healed as written in Isaiah 53:5."

The police advised me to make the report the next day in Des Plaines, Illinois. I did so.

I was discouraged with having a second incident in the same year. I continued to pray, since the first and second incidents began playing in my dreams. I learned that I needed to plead the blood of Jesus over my sleep before bedtime in order to have a peaceful night's rest.

Remember that the devil wants us to be distraught. <u>Incidents in our lives build faith and prayer stamina.</u> However, the devil does not want us to use these incidents as stepping stones, rather complaining stones. Complaining keeps us from God's grace and glory. Complaining blocks our intended communion with God. <u>Do not complain.</u> Rather praise God for deliverance, even if the problem is not totally resolved. Each praise moves us closer to the desired prayer outcome!

I saw God's great deliverance again. I stayed home from work the next day. I saw the naprapath again. I returned to work on November 3, 2004. I knew that God had undertaken for me, since I was able to continue with my daily activities.

After a couple of naprapathic visits, I was feeling better and kept praising God. Darnell and I rebuked accidents and thanked God for His angelic cover for our lives. According to Psalm 91:11, "For he shall give his angels charge over me to keep me in all of my ways."

On November 23, 2004, the Lord advised me to cook one of my two (2) turkeys for Thanksgiving. I considered the thought and cooked one turkey not knowing that the next day someone else would crash into my van.

Incident Three

The night of November 24, 2004 was icy and snowy. I asked God for protection as I left work. The path to the expressway was moving slowly. I saw the vehicle coming quickly. I prayed again that God would slow the driver. The driver appeared to be moving faster than everyone else. He struck the rear end of my van.

We pulled off of the main road to call the police. They asked that we come to the Police Station within the next week. We made plans to do so. As we exchanged information; it turned out that this man was a co-worker.

He told me that he had not thought that he needed to slow down, because it did not appear that icy to him. This statement helps us all to pray for drivers that feel the conditions do not warrant them doing anything differently. As always, I pray for safe trips and ask God to assist all drivers in maneuvering their cars.

The pain started again in my left lower back. I kept repeating out loud as I drove home that "God's stripes healed me". I held my head all the way home. I took a warm bath and slept. The next day was difficult. My husband and son helped me with lifting the roaster in and out of the oven. My daughter helped make the side dishes. I was glad that I started things on Tuesday. Otherwise, Thanksgiving would have been missing the main dish for dinner, since I annually make the turkeys for a gathering of approximately twenty-five (25) for my husband's family.

I learned that God does not give us details but He does give us opportunities to obey.

Incident Four

On December 12, 2004, as I left the grocery store, a car pulled up on the left and would not clear the thoroughfare. I beckoned the driver to go ahead. I waited for about five (5) minutes.

I then checked my left side mirror, and saw the car that was parallel to me. Nothing was coming; I moved into the street cautiously. The other driver was waiting for my space that is why they did not move when I motioned for the driver to move beyond my area on the street.

As I moved forward, a third car appeared suddenly. We collided. This was another incident! I told the Lord that I knew He was a protector and that the devil could not prevail in my life.

I called the police and the insurance company. I prayed that both the other lady driver and I would be fine because "by his stripes we **all** are healed".

Neither car was severely damaged. I prayed with my husband again upon arrival home for God's deliverance from these types of incidents.

I do praise God today that He gave me a mind to continue on with my life, in spite of how I felt on certain days. I praise Him for the sustaining power of His mercy. He **proved** repeatedly that with "**fully persuaded faith**" any of us can conquer challenges in life with God's sustaining power.

Prayer Jewels:

1) "Cast thy burden upon the LORD, and he shall sustain thee: he shall never suffer the righteous to be moved, Psalms 55:22.

2) "But he was wounded for our transgressions; he was bruised for our iniquities: the chastisement of our peace was upon him; and with **his stripes** we are **healed,** Isaiah 53:5.

3) "For he shall give his angels charge over you to keep me in all of your ways," Psalm 91:11.

CHAPTER FOUR

Tested and Delivered Again

Enter new bank players from Charlotte, North Carolina in 2007…

My husband's bank was under the radar to be sold. The deal went through, but it needed to be confirmed by the European legislature during the summer of 2007.

Waiting again…will the bank be sold or will it not be? If it was sold, employees were thinking what would their fate be?

One thing **always** occurs with waiting: we get to know God more deeply when we use Philippians 4:7 as a mascot anchor. "The peace of God that passes all understanding" can saturate any feelings of discomfort or anxiousness that waiting brings.

We all know that waiting feels like we are aimlessly stomping and kicking leaves on a fall day. Waiting feels like we are perspiring on a 100 degree day. Waiting tries our patience. Waiting carries emotional trouble; God's magnificent peace supersedes the anxiousness associated with waiting. Glory to God!

A couple of months passed. The answer was prepared for new owners and new challenges. Next, employees were advised to prepare for interviews during fall 2007. No one knew what jobs were open. The job posting board did not show anything that met my husband's skills.

However, God was at work again on our behalf. My husband's interview was scheduled for Thursday morning, November 1, 2007 originally. The day and time changed to Friday, November 2, 2007.

He **looked again** at the job posting board Thursday afternoon, November 1, 2007. This time, he saw a job for a Data Risk Manager. The posting needed a person with IT (computer knowledge) and project management skills. An exact match…that was orchestrated by God!

The interview started out with the usual questions about the one (1) and five (5) year career plans. When my husband mentioned the specific job posting, the course of the interview changed.

The job reported directly to the VP that did the interview! Imagine the next part of God's divine orchestration…his current boss interviewed immediately after him. His current manager confirmed that my husband was a diligent worker and was an asset to the department. The Senior VP left with a good impression.

My husband learned during the next two (2) weeks that he did not need to do the phone interview with Human Resources nor with the immediate departmental manager as he was initially told! He was the "top candidate!"

God gloriously positioned him for transition again!

Prayer Jewels:

1) Each challenge places us on another platform to anticipate God's deliverance with more victory in our hearts. Pray deliberately for His will and success.

2) Look again. Do not give up; press toward the mark of the high calling in God as Paul did in Philippians 3:14.

CHAPTER FIVE

※

Preparing for Lay-offs

In September 2000, all employees at our company were called to an extraordinarily large meeting that was set-up in the company warehouse. This type of meeting had never been held before.

The announcement made us aware that over the next three (3) years, 2001, 2002 and 2003 jobs would be moved to other lower cost areas in the U. S. and Puerto Rico away from Chicago, IL. All were shocked and surprised. I began to pray, since I was not sure how this announcement would affect me in carrying out my position as Nurse Manager.

Our Grand Avenue Warehouse employees were first on the list to go. Employees from that facility were clearly more sad than employees from other facilities leaving in either 2002 or 2003, due to the immediacy of the departure dates.

Human Resources advised me that I would be one of the partners on the Career Transition Team. I wondered what this meant, since I was the nurse.

It was a wonderful opportunity to assist employees in resume preparation, interviewing and witnessing for God, though.

I had numerous encounters with distraught employees regarding their futures. With their permission, I was able to encourage them that God **always** provides. Several employees asked me to pray for "the next steps" in their lives. The individuals and I prayed; the answers were gratifying for them.

Miracle One

Workers from Grand Avenue felt frustrated with supervisors and managers for many things from the past, prior to the announcement. It reminded me of Jesus telling Martha that she was "cumbered (burdened or overloaded) with many things" when her sister, Mary, did not help her serve Jesus during his visit to their house, St. Luke 10: 39-42.

An outcome of this frustration was that an employee presented the idea to shoot a supervisor and manager to me because of overloading with assignments. The employee felt that discrimination had occurred. Therefore, the employee had purchased a gun with bullets and had these items in the trunk. The employee identified the persons for the intended shooting early one morning in the Employee Health Services Department.

(Be aware that a well-thought plan increases the probability of the attack).

I prayed for very quickly and quietly for God's wisdom. I called the Employee Assistance Program (EAP) that our job offered. I asked for a counselor to be **immediately assigned** to me for this issue. The EAP Intake Worker advised me that she would call the "on duty" counselor immediately. I was surprised to hear about these intentions, since I knew the employee to be level-headed.

That day, God kept giving me words of wisdom to calm the employee down during the six (6) hours that we waited for direct contact with the counselor.

I had the employee rest on the departmental cot and I checked on the employee every half hour. The employee offered many reasons to leave to finish all daily tasks, yet the employee stayed until we received the call.

Note: the Department had one private room with a cot, an area with a large sink to cleanse onsite injuries, a bathroom with wheelchair access, and two (2) office desks in a U-shape format and another room for files and a desk for the administrative support with a door plus a phone.

I really believe that the employee was cooperative because the young person knew that an intervention was needed to detour any performance of potentially fatal actions. I was not expecting to confront this type of situation; however, I was **very glad** that I had followed the Lord's instructions to pray each day at the entry gates of the company for peaceful interactions as soon as I learned that we were preparing to depart through lay-offs, according to Psalm 133:1:

"Indeed, it is good and pleasant it is for brethren (co-workers) to dwell and (to depart) together in unity! " (Parentheses are mine).

I convinced the employee that this was very serious and that no one wanted trouble with the police from actually shooting the management team. The employee grunted and said, "You're right".

The counselor finally called with apologetic words for the long delay. Another emergency had occurred which took several hours to unravel.

The counselor spoke with the employee for about one hour in an adjacent, private room with the cot inside the Employee Health Services Office. I continued to pray; I alerted management since the employee was not within my direct presence.

The counselor convinced the employee to go to the hospital for treatment that afternoon. The counselor made hospital arrangements and needed me to initiate the short term disability process within the company for this employee. I did so.

I inquired of the counselor what the plan of action should be regarding this employee leaving the premise with the alleged bullets and unloaded gun in the car.

The counselor advised me to call the police with this information and alert the management team along with facility security. I did call the police and gave the license plate number as well as gave updates to the management team. The counselor felt that the employee would go quietly to the hospital admissions office. This is indeed what happened. Praise God!

The employee was hospitalized for several weeks. Upon discharge, the employee requested an early severance package. This was granted and the employee left peaceably without any harm to other employees. Praise God!

In the middle of these lay-off discussions and preparation, God blessed me to assist my sister-in-law, Marva Mahone, with her clinical graduate studies in nursing for North Park University. I served as the adjunct faculty/preceptor for her and other students during 2001.

Miracle Two

My good friend at work, Loretta Wilson, received notice that her "off payroll" date would be November 15, 2002. We prayed diligently that God would provide a job for her, especially since she was a single parent with three small (3) children.

Loretta searched the job postings for the Corporate and Rolling Meadows facilities. No jobs were open immediately. She searched again and again. We continued to pray fervent prayers with praise for God's mercy each week. On Thursday, November 14, 2002, God supplied the request! Loretta received a call that she was the leading candidate for the job in "Formula Control" in the Rolling Meadows Facility. She started the following Monday on November 18, 2002. Praise God for His great **on-time** faithfulness!

The irony of the job title is the God controls all formulas; yes, He does!

Miracle Three

Another office worker had an "off payroll" date in November 2002. He was a tithe-paying, fervent Christian; God supplied a job for him within five (5) days of his release date! We praised God for His great deliverance!

Miracle Four

I was originally had an "off payroll" date of December 31, 2002. During the summer of 2002, Human Resources approached me with an offer to transfer to the Distribution Center that was located within two miles of the main building. I sought the Lord on this issue with my husband and prayer friends.

I agreed to the transfer and worked there from January 2 through September 26, 2003. I began interviewing for other jobs in May 2003; none suited my interests. On the jobs that I was originally offered, the pay was cut by 38%. I kept asking God for a job that was befitting to my interests and had better pay. The pay at the job that I took at Motorola was closer to my original salary.

I interviewed with Motorola in Schaumburg, IL. I was the fourth candidate. The hiring manager advised me that this position might not be favorable, since others had interviewed previously with the "Team".

I told her, "It does not matter which position I had during the interview process, first, second, third or fourth. God gives favor and that's what I need." I always ask for favor with God and man, according to St. Luke 2:52:

"And Jesus increased in wisdom and stature, and in favor with God and man".

The "Team" needed time to discuss their points of view about the "proper fit" of each candidate. She promised to call me during the last week of September. This happened to be the week that I would be off-payroll.

As I prepared to finish my tour of duty, I planned fall flu shot clinics at remaining facilities throughout the Chicagoland area. This meant that I was not at my work location throughout the day for two (2) consecutive days.

I missed the offer calls. The hiring manager called my husband at home on Thursday, September 25, 2003. He gave her my personal cell number. I called her back that afternoon. No answer.

On my last day, I needed to transfer email files to Human Resources. I tried to do so for two (2) hours. The computer needed rebooting several times.

I called the company Help Desk. They had trouble getting the files to move also.

At 9:45 a.m., I received a call from the hiring manager, she offered me the job! I was overwhelmed with God's faithfulness and provision! He made sure that I **knew** that I had another position before the old one ended! How great is our God!

Miracle Five

A Distribution Center employee, Martin Estrada, hurt his finger at work early in January 2003. He saw the company doctor and needed to get daily dressing changes in the Employee Health Services office. During those dressing changes, he asked for specific prayers to bridge his service for his pension.

The pension eligibility date was October 2003. He had an "off payroll" date for August 2003. Martin asked for prayer that would act as a bridge to cross into October.

I told him that I would pray and ask others to join us for the manifestation of this request. Martin stated that he knew I believed God; therefore, he felt this level of faith would get the job done! We prayed many times at lunch for God to show His power; Martin inquired with upper management about opportunities to reach his pension eligibility. Denials came until late August 2003.

Martin got an extension beyond August 31 when he was needed to assist the maintenance workers in the Rolling Meadows Facility on special project!

Then, the Distribution Center had another major transition project for floor cleaning and breaking down the warehouse racking. The project lasted into October 2003!

God did it! I had never seen God do something of this magnitude! My faith was increased!

Prayer Jewels:

1) "Wait on the Lord: be of good courage", Psalm 27:14.

2) When files do not transfer, check what God's purpose is.

3) "The effective, fervent prayer of the righteous avails much", James 5:16.

CHAPTER SIX

Dwight's Great Deliverances

On Sunday afternoon, May 13, 2001, God reminded me to input all of my praying friends' phone numbers in my cell. I thought about it and said to myself, "I don't really need to do this, since I know all of the numbers by heart." The thought came repeatedly. I finally added several numbers with Melissa's help.

I had to attend early morning meetings in Rolling Meadows on Tuesday, May 15, 2001. I prayed with my husband as we customarily did before going to work. I had prayed for Melissa (our daughter), earlier in the morning. Dwight was still asleep; I asked my husband to pray for him before he left for a 9 a.m. school start, since I had not had the chance.

I arrived in Rolling Meadows at 7:30 a.m. I completed both meetings by 8:30 a.m. and I was preparing to return to my home facility. One of the Administrative Support employees in the Rolling Meadows, paged me for a call from my office. The message was, "Call home".

I tried calling my husband at home, but there was no answer. I called him on his cell phone; there was also no answer. I called my office; my Administrative Support, Lisa Audiffred, told me that Dwight had been struck by a car. Another person was also struck. No one knew the severity;

my husband was en route to the West Suburban Hospital with Dwight in the ambulance.

I felt such a surge of anxiety! Then, I remembered my scriptures in Philippians 4: 6-8 that I had been reading every day since 1996. "Be anxious for nothing; make my request known unto God". Offer thanksgiving, **the missing ingredient,** for unanswered prayers.

I tried to collect myself to drive back to the city. It would be over an hour's drive with the morning's rush hour traffic. I thought, "How can I stay calm enough to drive all the way there by myself?"

Then, I thought about all the programmed numbers! I started calling my praying friends instantly with "my request" for Dwight, my husband and me.

I reached several Christians easily. One of which was Sister Betsy Bullis. I remember vividly what Sister Betsy prayed, "Dear Lord, we have a request for Dwight's safety and healing. Please assist him right now, in Jesus' name. He will not need a cane, walker, crutch nor wheel chair, by the blood of Jesus. He is whole right now and so is the other person with him. We declare the Word of God. When Sister Marilynn gets to the hospital, she simply parks because Dwight and her husband are ready to go back home because Dwight is discharged. We believe what we pray in Jesus' name."

Sister Betsy encouraged me to remain calm as I drove. I kept thanking God that my husband and I were faithful tithers. Therefore, "the devourer would be rebuked for our sakes", as Malachi 3: 10-11 stated. I repeated this over and over. I kept asking God to give me strength to focus on driving. How I wished for a chauffer during that hour ride!

I parked in the four-tiered parking lot on the highest floor. I went to the emergency room to look for Dwight and my husband. I saw Dwight first.

Dwight was concerned that his brand new jeans had to be cut by the paramedics to check the status of his right thigh and hip, since he struck the windshield and the ground after he was flipped in the air by the taxi.

My husband was concerned about getting them home, since he had called a taxi and the taxi went to the other hospital entrance, then left. My husband was relieved to see me, since the taxi had just departed. He asked me to go to retrieve the car so we could go home. Dwight was just discharged. **No broken bones!** He had a contusion the size of a grapefruit on the right side of his temple and multiple abrasions. God was very good to him that day!

When we arrived at home, my husband advised me that he had just prayed for Dwight before he left for school; he got a call from the crossing guard stating that Dwight had been struck. Then, I began an arduous process of picking minute pieces of shattered glass out of his head. This took between 30-45 minutes.

Next, Dwight asked for food.

I made lunch since it was 11:30 a.m. I asked my husband to agree with me in prayer for the grapefruit-sized contusion to disintegrate by 6 p.m. that day. We asked God's blessings in Jesus' name and anointed Dwight with blessed olive oil. He ate then slept for several hours.

When Dwight awakened around 5:30 p.m., the contusion was only the size of a small lemon! Praise God! He ate and continued improving.

We saw the doctor the next day. He had other x-rays. Everything was fine; Dwight was bruised and limping. He remained out of school for two (2) days.

Dwight's friend had a contusion to his foot; he got crutches. Joshua returned to school the next day. Joshua's mom called to state, "my boy was covered with your boy's blessing. Neither of them was killed."

Dwight and Joshua had crossed in the middle of the street en route to the Shell gas station before school. Both walked through the alley from our street and proceeded toward their destination. Neither paid attention to the left turning lane; the taxi had entered the lane to turn left. The driver alleged he did not see them.

The Assistant Principal, Mrs. Robinstine, witnessed the incident and said, "Mrs. James, you should have seen **how high** Dwight flipped into the air! All of the students and teachers on street patrol feared he was dead after the impact. The eyewitnesses heard the impact".

Mrs. Robinstine told all of the onlookers that Dwight was from a praying family. "If anyone would survive, it would be Dwight. The family could take this kind of hit and survive!" I heard what she said and just praised God that our lights had shined at the junior high school. Mrs. Robinstine commended me for praying on issues with her job previous to the day of the incident.

Prayer Jewels:

1) This taught me the power of continuing in pray in an emergency!

2) Also, it is necessary to touch and agree with believing saints.

3) Do **not** leave home **without** prayer.

The Next Great Deliverance

On Saturday, June 12, 2004, Dwight came home for lunch from his part-time job at Kentucky Fried Chicken in Westchester, IL. We talked briefly; he said that he was scheduled to work until midnight. He would call when he got into his car to head home. The car was two (2) days in

Dwight's possession as a tool to get him to and from work. My husband and I had blessed the car upon delivery to him.

Sixteen year old Dwight descended down the front stairs to the street. I called him back to me at the front door to pray for his safety. Dwight's reply was, "Mom, you prayed for me already this morning as you always do."

I told him, "Dwight, it hits me to pray for you again for safety. I don't know why. Come back." We prayed; Dwight departed.

It was a hot summer day. I had a lot of errands that day, so I went to bed before 8:30 p.m. This early prep for bedtime was unusual. I slept **very** soundly.

My husband got a call from the Chicago Police at little after 8:30 p.m. informing him that Dwight had been side-swiped on Austin Boulevard by another driver that appeared under the influence of something.

My husband went to the site a few blocks from home and waited for a long time as the Chicago and Oak Park Police decided to which jurisdiction the incident belonged. Austin is a dividing street between Chicago and Oak Park.

The mosquitoes were prevalent; my husband had many bites when he came home. Dwight was struck in the late model Jetta on the driver's side. The driver's side door collapsed and bent into the middle of the car from the impact. All of the driver's window glass shattered and went into the window shaft. The windshield shattered and had multiple places where the long lines formed.

Dwight and the other male driver declined to go to the hospital. Dwight had bruises on his left thigh, not one cut from all of the shattered glass! The other driver was taken into custody by the police and given a ticket.

When I awakened in the morning, my husband and the children cautioned me not to panic when I saw the remnants of the car. My husband had it towed to our garage at home until the insurance company could inspect it.

I was horrified when I saw that the driver's door was very dented and bent into the middle of the car to the passenger's side! I quickly asked Dwight how he got out of the car. His reply was, "Mom, I just crawled out on the passenger side!" He was so nonchalant about it. Dwight had a slight contusion by his left thigh, which we prayed would be dissolved. It disappeared by the power of God! When I saw all of the glass from the window on the driver's side inside the car, I was amazed that he did not have any lacerations!

I quickly remembered the second call to Dwight and I told my husband what happened. God wanted Dwight to have extra prayer coverage for the evening's events before he left for work. How I praise God for following that leading of the Lord! Yes, I truly praise Him for helping me obey that unction to pray the second time!

Since Kentucky Fried had slow business the past evening, Dwight got off around 8 p.m., instead of 12 midnight. He took a co-worker home and consequently was on Austin and not in Westchester, IL.

My husband remarked that I was in Rolling Meadows for the taxi incident and asleep for the car issue. I told him that God wanted to insulate me from the actual events. Each time, we had prayed for Dwight. I really praise God for the power of prayer.

Prayer Jewels:

1) Pray again, even if you do not know why, when <u>God's unction</u> comes over you.

2) Do not skip blessing new vehicles. Angels are dispatched.

3) Do <u>not</u> leave home <u>without</u> prayer.

CHAPTER SEVEN

Melissa's Angel

Melissa was very shy from grade school through high school. Darnell and I had continually prayed for Melissa's confidence to blossom by the end of high school.

Enter Mr. Peter Kahn, high school English teacher! He has ties with London, England and throughout Chicago in the poetry world. Mr. Kahn heads the Spoken Word Poetry Program at Oak Park and River Forest High School.

Melissa had the opportunity to participate in any of the three (3) annual showcases during her sophomore and junior years of high school. Mr. Kahn connected with 50-54 students for each showcase to expertly write poems with a great insight into their young lives.

This mode of expression was perfect for Melissa! She could synthesize her thoughts in private, practice her poem with trusted friends and then muster courage to perform the poem on stage. Many friends and family witnessed her poetic talents and encouraged Melissa to continue to build her skills.

Each time Melissa's group performed, Melissa would have a lapse of memory regarding her lines. However, God's grace saturated her confidence so that the lapses became words, not complete sentences. In the past, Melissa would have shrunk down to pulverized particles with any lapses such as these. Melissa was unflappable with her new friends.

At each performance, Melissa's confidence unfolded like petals on a flower. Spoken Word is a widely known avenue for our youth to showcase their voice through original words and ideas inspired by the work of professional poets. The support from family and friends was a much needed part of her metaphoric talents.

The most beneficial interactions have emanated from the London Exchange Students. Melissa acted as a hostess on numerous occasions. Every October, the London students visit Oak Park, IL to participate in the Annual Fall Spoken Word Club Showcase. Of course, this meant that Darnell and I were chauffeurs.

Melissa's excitement would swell as the students emailed prior to their visits. When the students visit, they have structured events like breakfast at the Oak Park Original Pancake House each year. They also take public transportation. Melissa has not necessarily preferred this mode of transportation. God's healing grace rode the local trains with her and the group. God is so merciful! Many times, we have praised Mr. Kahn for his kindness to Melissa and unassuming presentation style that he taught all of the students.

The Exchange Students have been so excited to see Oak Park houses, the malls and the movies in America. Melissa became very comfortable with introducing many students in succession. She did not stammer nor await others to introduce themselves.

In Melissa's senior year in High School she mentored a new protégé to the Spoken Word Club. Melissa has also continued to volunteer with the Spoken Word Club and chaperone the students from England.

Prayer Jewels:

1) Keep praying for God to dispatch the "angel" that is needed for your family. Do not give up. Many Mr. Kahn(s) are there; we need to draw them to the situations for service by prayer.

2) Pray for those who are assigned to your family, like the ancillary London visitors who were assigned to Melissa. Pray for God to bring them to your family sooner than later.

CHAPTER EIGHT

Mom's Surprise

On Friday, March 10, 2006, my older sister Linda Owens-Jackson called me to advise me that she was accompanying our mom to Loyola Hospital's Emergency Room in Maywood, IL for back pain. I called several times during the night to check on her status. No status was given.

By 7 a.m. on March 11, 2006, I called Linda to ask if she wanted me to relieve her. Linda stated that she preferred to stay. Later in the morning, I went to the hospital after mom was admitted to the hospital.

Mom kept saying that she had back pain. We prayed for her. Linda left. I did not say much nor stay long, since she was tired. Linda and Mom had been up all night.

I visited several days in a row. Her legs swelled; compression hose were added on Tuesday, March 14, 2006. Still no mention was made of her real issue. I asked the Christians across the nation to join us in prayer for this severe "back pain".

On Thursday, March 16, 2006, the Lord tugged at me all morning to go to the hospital at lunch, since my job was close by the hospital. I brought soup for lunch for both of us.

Mom was not able to eat it because she was **"not responsive"**, when I arrived at the hospital. The doctors kept saying that she was "not responsive". We had **not** been notified of this point during the morning.

I began to pray, text-message and call my siblings and prayer friends to agree for her ability to live through the day. I asked God to keep her in the land of the living, since our father died in April 2005. As a family, we were **not** ready for her demise.

Let me explain further why we were unprepared for her demise. Our father died in the year prior, after he lived with one kidney from 1983-2005. During the last two (2) weeks of his life he was on dialysis, much to his dismay.

Our father had been afflicted with pneumonia and bronchitis many times, gout and hypertension. A bout with shingles left him unable to fully smile in 2000. (Shingles is a form of chickenpox that can affect the nerves in the torso and face). This was emotionally painful for him since he was jolly and loved people.

Our family experienced many hospitalizations and negative "he may not live through the night" reports for over 22 years past the loss of his kidney in 1983.

We were still adjusting to his departure; I knew that I needed to pray profoundly and deeply for God's intervention for Mom. The doctors told me that she had cancer which was the cause of her back pain, due to metastasis. This hospitalization was not only about treating back pain, but cancer also. **What a surprise!** The doctors were not expecting her to make it through the day!

I heard this news over and over again and began to quote and read Isaiah 53: 1-5. It states that we believe the report of the Lord. I told the devil that was the only report and status that we needed. I anointed Mom with blessed (olive) oil and kept telling her that by Jesus' stripes she was effectively healed. Over and over, I repeated this to her for eight (8) hours. It did not appear that she even heard me.

The other siblings, my husband and my nephew, Brandon, came later in the afternoon and evening. We all prayed again. Finally, mom showed signs of revival. She made it through that night and remained with us the next year and nine months. Glory to God! Mom told me two (2) weeks later that she also had thought that March 16, 2006 was her last day on earth.

I trusted God that day like never before; my faith grew that day! I held onto His Word like never before for eight (8) hours. I realized how important it is to trust Him all day and all night.

The next approximate two (2) years were very difficult. Mom had radiation therapy for her back and cancer condition during August and September 2006. Marva Mahone, my sister-in-law, my husband, Darnell, Korveeta Mahone, my youngest sister, and I took the brunt of transportation calls to these visits.

She had a surgery to place a stent in her lungs to fight off blood clots; Mom did not have any complications with the surgery, although Mom was very concerned about the surgery. Mom rejoiced abundantly when she saw all of us post-operatively, since she knew that she had lived through the procedure!

Mom lived with our oldest sister, Linda, for several months post-discharge as she re-gained her strength and stamina. Our brother-in-law, Tomie Jackson, was **very** hospitable to Mom. He made breakfast and assisted her wherever he could. This is particularly important since he was 86+ years old at this time. Mom ultimately went back to her house on October 31, 2006; she was self-sufficient through August 2007. The four oldest children made frequent visits to her house to assure that she was okay and to carry items that she needed.

I am the second oldest child. Wayne is the third child; he has been a great anchor in assisting Mom after her legs failed her. His strength made the difference for her.

Korveeta, the fourth child, planned a vacation during July and August 2007 to Detroit, Michigan and Canada. I encouraged Mom to go; she wavered about making the trip. She decided to go and asked me to pack for her. Korveeta made the hotel and car rental arrangements for the church convention. Linda and Tomie drove separately to the same convention. Mom and Korveeta had physical challenges while she was away.

Linda and Tomie had to buy her a wheel chair because her legs did not support her as fully as Mom needed at the convention site, since there were long distances to walk. Mom had a bout of vomiting; hence she did not stay at church service as long anticipated.

On the final day of their vacation, Korveeta and Mom crossed the border into Canada for a couple of hours; Mom had long desired to go to Canada. Korveeta thought that she strained her leg as she brought the luggage down the stairs at the hotel. Therefore, Mom assisted Korveeta in the drive back. Mom's stamina was sufficient to drive at least 200 miles. What glory!

During her illness, Darnell and I did relay car trips with Mom every two weeks to the hair salon after she was released from the hospital in 2006. Darnell dropped her off on his way from work; I picked her up as I came from work and French-braided her hair at my house after dinner. The last such hair styling trip was Thursday, August 23, 2007, after Korveeta and Mom returned from their Detroit trip.

As Mom descended the stairs at my house to go to the garage, her knees buckled. I asked what happened. She said, "This happens sometimes." I advised her to call her doctor as soon as possible the next morning, since this was an unusual occurrence that warranted medical review. Mom called the doctor. The doctor wanted her to be seen in the emergency room, since she had slid down to the floor around 5 a.m. the morning of August 24, 2007. Mom had not broken any bones during this slide incident.

Wayne, the oldest son, took her to the ER. She was released from the emergency room with an instruction to call the family doctor on Tuesday, August 28, 2007. Wayne took her to the doctor on the following Tuesday. Mom was admitted for further testing about her condition. Dr. Lo determined that the tumor had invaded the thoracic spinal cord.

I called Cornelius, our youngest brother, to advise him about this finding relating to Mom's condition. Cornelius told me that he knew already. Linda, the oldest, had informed him. Cornelius was house-bound at that time due to his diagnosis of muscular sclerosis. This disease affected his muscles and nerves progressively; this meant that Cornelius could not sit up nor walk at that time.

More radiation was ordered for Mom. It was ordered to start during Labor Day week in 2007. We prayed for God's answer. We could not lift her into and out of any of our cars anymore. We needed an ambulance to transport Mom; however, the hospital staff said that this would not be approved by Medicare. Next, the hospital staff decided to release her to Linda's home again on September 5, 2007.

Wayne took her back on Friday, September 7, 2007, for a check-up. Mom was admitted to the hospital due to the swelling and immobility of her legs. More radiation was ordered. An ambulance took her each day from her hospital room to the Oncology Radiation Department. What an interesting answer to prayer!

Mom spent her birthday on September 10, 2007 in the hospital. Coincidentally, Andre, the High School Security Officer was at the hospital with his mom. He came in to visit Mom and told her, "Marilynn walked around the High School for years praying for the children rain or snow. We always laughed at her. She just kept prayer walking. Her kids are out of high school, though. I want her to pray for my mom who is in the room next to yours."

Andre requested prayer for his mom, since she was hospitalized with a leg fracture past a fall. Her birthday was on September 26, 2007. I was privileged to pray with his mom.

Mom stayed in the hospital and was later transferred to Renaissance Rehabilitation Center. There was much deliberation about where she would be transferred. I checked out a nursing and rehabilitation home in Westchester, IL. Linda and Wayne evaluated Renaissance Rehabilitation Center in Hillside, IL. All three of us visited Columbus Park Rehabilitation Center in Chicago, IL. The main issue was the ability for the center to care for Mom's rehabilitation needs and travel convenience/expressway proximity for us, since all four of us continued working full time. Cornelius' Multiple Sclerosis grew worse so he was hospitalized and sent to rehabilitation simultaneously to Mom's final months.

Collectively, none of us wanted to place Mom in any center, since this would signal her decreased independence. All of us knew that Mom **prided** herself in being able to take care of herself and handle her business.

Mom voiced her concern to Korveeta, "Where are they going to put me?" Korveeta related her reply, "Mom, they will look for a center that will address your needs." Per Korveeta, that settled the issue for that time.

Mom got therapy six days per week for several weeks at Renaissance Rehabilitation Center; the goal was to build her up the upper arms and overall strength for pushing her wheelchair.

Mom gave Korveeta, Wayne, Linda and me many requests for food and fruit. Marva, Wayne's wife, made dinner for her several times. When we visited, Mom met us at the elevator in her wheelchair. Her tenacity penetrated every family visit. Mom still wanted us to know that she was in control.

I gave her a shower every Saturday afternoon and French-braided her hair. Korveeta spent Sunday afternoons with her and brought her favorite food — chicken. Wayne went with her to the hospital for doctors' visits while she was in Renaissance. Linda kept up with the doctors' status summaries. Praise God that we had several siblings and that we were all local!

Then, Mom started coughing as she sat in her wheelchair Friday, November 16, 2007 as she prepared to go back to Linda's house during the Department of Aging Case Manager Nurse's intake visit. I advised the Rehab Nurse and called Linda. I asked for a chest x-ray.

Linda followed up on Saturday morning. I saw the x-ray technician as I left on Saturday, November 17, 2007. Linda checked again on Sunday, November 18, 2007 for the results. The x-ray was positive for pneumonia. Linda persisted to get a doctor's order for hospital transfer, since Linda had Power of Attorney.

Once Mom was back at the hospital, she was bedridden from this point forward. On Wednesday, November 21, 2007, Mom told me that we had our prayers answered. She had a life extension as requested and stated that she was tired. Mom asked me if I knew the prayers were answered. I replied, "Yes, we did have our prayers answered." I told her that I released her. Mom was quiet. I left shortly thereafter.

The next day was Thanksgiving; Darnell and I visited her. She was glad to see us early in the morning. Korveeta came in shortly thereafter. We all praised God for His goodness that we were in the land of the living!

On Friday, November 23, 2007, Linda called me to advise that Mom was placed into the **Hospice Program** at Loyola. Doctors told Linda that day that Mom had a few weeks to live. Mom would be sent home immediately on Saturday, November 24, 2007, to Linda's house, since she could not be alone. I saw Mom with Linda and Korveeta that Friday night.

The next morning, Mom called me about 8:05 a.m. She was in distress regarding her pain medicine; she had not received it through the night as ordered. I finished dressing and went with Darnell to see her. Mom was **very distressed** from her sleeping medicine from Friday night. Her demeanor was **very agitated.**

We tried to calm her several times. Darnell and I prayed again. The nurse got the pharmacy issue corrected and gave Mom the pain medicine. Mom went to sleep for a couple of hours; Darnell and I went to the hospital cafeteria for lunch.

We awaited the ambulance for the afternoon transport to Linda's house. Mom got to Linda's house and rejoiced. When Tomie made lunch for her, Mom began crying.

Linda went to get more things needed for her; Darnell and I got her medicine from Walgreen's. Korveeta, Wayne and Linda did on night calls with Mom for the next week and a half.

On Monday, November 26, 2007, Mom was discomfited as I manned the daytime shift with her. She did not want to eat or talk much. She had a fever; I kept offering her cool compresses. After the seventh or eighth time, Mom passed the cloth back to me and went to sleep for a couple of hours.

When Mom awakened, she told me that "Everyone over there was happy! Everyone over there was happy! They were dancing and singing. I joined them while they were dancing; I showed them how to dance. Some were 100, 200 and 300 years old. I was too young to be with them. I came back because I saw all of you back here crying. I made a decision; I came back to help you. Do you know when I will transition?"

I responded, "No".

She then called Tomie. "Deacon Tomie, do you know when my transition is?" He thought for a moment and replied, "Those transitions are variable". Thank God for an 87 year old answer.

Later that Monday, Korveeta came. She asked Korveeta the same question. I replied, "When a person has an opportunity to ask about transitioning, clearly the transition is not now. Usually, a person transitions and no one knows it." Mom nodded her head and did not ask the question anymore.

Korveeta began praying for Mom to be made whole; she prayed so fervently that my faith increased again!

Mom ate very well the next morning; she called me early! Korveeta and Linda were so ecstatic!

Mom was up and down the rest of the week. All of the grandchildren visited. Dwight and Brandon Mahone were so helpful with lifting her from her bed into the chair or wheelchair when needed.

On Sunday, December 2, 2007, Linda called Wayne around 9 p.m. to assist her to get Mom to the table to eat, per Mom's request. However, she could not stay up very long; her hips were hurting. Per Linda, Mom had a lot of swelling in her hips that night. Wayne and Linda got her back into bed.

On Monday, December 3, 2007, Linda and the health aide gave her a bath in the early afternoon. Linda left for an appointment and Tomie remained with Mom.

Darnell asked me that evening at dinner "how was I?" I responded, "Very tired. I didn't see us carrying on this frantic pace much longer. Working a busy nursing job, household duties and Mom were beyond what I could imagine". I told him that I had learned that God's grace was sufficient over the past approximate two (2) years. I did not know that our journey with Mom was ending as I was answering Darnell at dinner.

Korveeta visited Mom at Linda's house around 8 p.m. that Monday night; she found Mom's old terrestrial body in the bed without her spirit.

Mom had put on the celestial body. Korveeta's call came just as I was donning my coat to go to visit Mom after dinner. I never saw her alive again.

We were all sad that night as we reminisced about her life and our journey during the past almost two (2) years. Linda and Korveeta reminisced about their many prayer times with Mom from Isaiah 53 and Jeremiah 17:14. We acknowledged that God had answered many prayers for us regarding her care. We were grateful. We knew that we would miss her. It seemed very strange to be in the world and not have either parent alive at that moment. Through these circumstances, we had been **fully persuaded** that God never fails!

Prayer Jewels:

1) Pray fervently until there is break-through; it may take several hours, days or years.

2) Pray for each family member's strength through a situation of this magnitude.

3) Pray for a good attitude as one cares for a family member.

4) Pray for all health care workers assigned to work cooperatively with family members and for positive interactions with all workers.

5) Pray for openings to witness to the health care workers involved.

6) Pray that trusted friends will under gird these care efforts with additional visits, telephone calls, cooking, cleaning, grocery shopping or assistance in other areas.

Our family doctor, Dr. Kenneth Blair, gave me a good piece of advice, which helped me cope early on with Mom's diagnosis and the late family notification of her situation: "Remember, none of us have control over another's grown person's choices regarding their treatment or lack thereof. Our job as the family member is to support the person during the crisis."

CHAPTER NINE

Reflections

As I review my steps lifetime-to-date, I know that I have pondered "why" I was at certain stages at certain times, especially when I arrived at the spot against my will. I always asked God "why me?"

What I have learned is God will give me one of three answers:

1) Silence — that is really tough because I have to pray more to ascertain and discern what God wants to happen.

2) Thundering words — this means that I need to do or not do something. What I do **not** like is hearing from God that I need to complete <u>yet another task</u> when I thought I was finished with the issue.

3) Soft words — this is God's way of encouraging me to stay strong to complete the good fight of faith.

<u>Understand</u> — God is not a God of dissertations and long speeches. He asks questions like, "did you do all that *you* can?" I always like to get on the side where I did all the things that I can think about doing. Then, I can easily and justifiably say, I did all. Now, I just "stand" as Ephesians 6:13 encourages.

However, *thinking* that I did all that God wanted done in a situation is not all that *I have needed to do.* It is *then* that I wanted God to figure it out and not me! That's where I have grown immensely.

Cases in Point

During my children's grade school through high school years, I did not like dealing with what I deemed as "silly" interactions with teachers and school administrators. For example, Melissa was a kinesthetic learner. She moved in her chair a lot in the primary grades. Calls from school to tell me that she moved in her chair were unnecessary to me. When I inquired if she disturbed other students the answer was always, "no". So, these types of calls left me in a quandary in terms of the teachers' desired solution and purpose of the calls.

In other situations, more investigation of accusations needed to be performed by the school system to get to the "heart of the matter". What my husband and I found was that there were two (2) sides to every story; assumptions were made without any probing or clarifying questions. These two (2) sides were determined by the part each party (student and teacher) played in the scenario. I did not like hearing that an investigation had occurred when the eyewitnesses had not ever been questioned. God would ask me to probe further. I did not necessarily desire to train others in their investigative duties. However, my children were usually exonerated when additional questions were asked. Often, there were no "eyewitnesses" to the charges. God wanted me to manage and restore the family name in accused spaces. In the books that I read, I had not seen Motherhood characterized as an episode from Colombo or Sherlock Holmes movies!

Also, I mistakenly believed that my husband and I would accurately know **"what happened"** when the adult on-the-scene summarized what occurred in their presence. That was not necessarily so. We encountered individual adults who either "did not remember", "did not want to recap" or "preferred not to convey" what actually happened. Yet, we were called to school in instances that made no sense in terms of the stated offense.

<u>**Consequently, I had to have a mega makeover to my belief system!**</u> That makeover assisted me in reducing my daily frustrations. My expectations and prayers changed.

Now, I pray for God's capital <u>"T"</u> truth for every interaction and situation. "Jesus is the way, the <u>truth</u> and the life", according to St. John 14: 6a. That prayer revelation has uncovered many un-investigated truths by God's radar in school and relational encounters. What I mean is sometimes truth must be sought **and** investigated, not just assumed and taken at face value.

What else happened as I joined prayer forces with many others? *I saw my faith abounding!* I remember God telling me that I did not **have** to have the same desire as a friend as stated in every prayer request; I just needed **to agree and believe** for the answer as I touched His throne with the requester. In other words, some things were not urgent for or to me, but the requester's heart was set to see God move in tandem with the request.

<u>**What did God teach me about myself?**</u> God showed me why He likes childlike faith. Childlike faith puts God at the helm and not us as adults.

People still believe today that I do not know when someone is mistreating, backdooring or excluding me. **I do know when those interactions occur.** However, God asks us to forgive. God has given me many opportunities to practice this grace.

I have proven what multiple forgiveness moments mean. When we determine to keep pure hearts as Matthews 5:8 states, we see God. We see God when we forgive after the next unkind incident and the next one. We see God developing Christian character and good reports through our lives.

Forgiving is a learned behavior, contrary to popular belief. The problem is that we prefer not to learn forgiveness and we prefer not to

practice this skill. We can not forgive on our own without God's direction and help. Forgiving is a choice!

Co-workers have told me that I really convicted their behavior because I did not mention how awful they treated me nor did I raise my voice when I should have been infuriated. They stated that they would have preferred my anger rather than my calm. The calm is from God; it was not my first choice since my youth.

I also want to highlight and put us all in remembrance that others see when we demonstrate and extend "patient understanding" to their situations and/or immature behaviors. Often, individuals need to "grow up" in successful communication and interaction skills, even though they are greater than eighteen (18) years old. When we model these skills, they grow!

Now, in my middle years, I appreciate God's faithfulness to my husband, my children, my family and me more than ever! I see His favor when my children were wrong at school and when the teachers were incorrect as well. I see how He kept us in trials, illnesses and dangerous moments. I see His direction in the professions we chose, now that offshoring is a common word in our vocabulary. I have seen His great deliverance and healing power over and over. I am privileged to have stood the test of faith for things that were indeed unseen at the time prayer requests were activated. Yet, now, in the following chapter, those manifested prayer requests are described. Glory to God!

How has God's faithfulness been most demonstrated to me? Although, it has not been easy balancing family and career, God has increased my flexibility and patience! I praise God because He has given me extreme strength to work and perform my family duties as well as be active in church. **Prayer answered equals faith increased.** Now, it feels comforting to know which prayer requests work effectively and efficiently.

What do I want God to do in the second half of my life? I want to see more of His faithfulness and participate in more ministry activities, such as mission trips that change or improve individuals' physical and spiritual lives. Also, I want to be at the helm of a prayer ministry with six (6) prayer ministers initially for those who have immediate or long term prayer requests. Expansion is always God's way as the ministry grows. I would like the privilege to stand with requesters until manifestation occurs. I believe that God will allow me to see these desires.

CHAPTER TEN

Testimonials: The Effectual Fervent Prayers of the Righteous Avail Much

This chapter will demonstrate the prayer connections that have made the difference in lives that were mentioned at the beginning of the book. Christians voluntarily and eagerly submitted summaries of the impact that fervent, continual prayer made as they went through transitions to higher ground in the Lord.

Sister Freda Robinson is a wife, the proud mother of five (5) and grandmother of three (3).

Per Sister Freda, "My faith was increased when I lost my job at a major customer service organization in 1996. I looked for a new job in New York. As I prepared to leave Illinois, Sister Marilynn gave me a prophetic word regarding my future in Chemistry".

Sister Marilynn told me, "Freda, be aware that you will move into management, get promoted, be bonus eligible and receive awards before these things ever happened to me.

Why are you saying that they will happen in the future, Sister Marilynn? This seems impossible!"

Sister Marilynn replied, "With God, all things are possible. Are you willing to pray and believe God with me for the same?" I answered, "Of course." We prayed and I left Chicago, bound for New York with my family and mom.

In 1997, after I was in New York for approximately 1.5 years, favor became a label on my life. I was promoted into management and I had employees reporting to me, as Sister Marilynn and I had prayed. I received awards from work that I did not know were submitted into the competition on my behalf! I was really grateful to God to see these prayers come to pass in my life.

What has most impacted me in my friendship with Marilynn and her family is the ongoing encouragement to be a better Christian in terms of praying regularly and fervently. I am personally more in contact with God, as a result of partnering with Marilynn in weekly fasting and prayer. I see the fruit in my life and my family's and the prosperity of possessing the firm rooting and grounding in the Word.

My prior experiences with Christians who had a prophetic cloak were not as positive, since some things stated came to pass and other things did not manifest. Now, I know that I have the gift of faith and the word of knowledge. These gifts have been passed down to me as I continued my friendship with Marilynn. I give God **all** the praise!

My son, Phillip, served in the Navy for six (6) years. While Iraq was being bombed from his ship, a bomb landed several feet from the ship. Phillip declined to tell me about it for over a year. He told me, "Mom, I knew that you, grandmother and Mrs. James were praying. I always prayed Psalm 91 while I served. Angels did protect me".

Prayer Jewel:

1) "But it is written, Eye has not seen nor ear heard, neither have entered into the heart of man, the things which god have prepared for them that love Him", I Corinthians 2:9!

Minister Al and Evangelist Ever Houston have been married for over forty (40) years. They are the parents of two, have a son-in-law and daughter-in-law plus one granddaughter.

During the late 1990's, Al moved a piece of machinery at work weighing between 500 and 600 pounds with a crane. The crane's cords slipped from the socket and the machine struck against both his hands. As a result of the incident, Al experienced an injury to both hands and wrists, which led to him developing carpal tunnel bilaterally. This injury also aggravated his degenerative arthritis.

Over the next two and a half years, Al had eight (8) surgeries to correct the issues that started with the hands and wrists. Both wrists were fused and bones were taken from the elbow to support the fusions. This procedure did not remain intact, so repeat surgeries were done with removal of hip bones for wrist stabilization.

After these bilateral surgeries, Al was left with minimal use of his hands and wrists and for a period of time. The prognosis was poor that Al would ever use his hands productively again, per the doctors' reports. He needed assistance with routine tasks that many of us take for granted, like feeding and dressing himself. But God already had the answer. During this same time period, Ever was laid off from a job where she had been a model employee. Yet, what the devil meant for bad, God used for their good. The layoff actually afforded Ever the free time she needed to be able to care for Al and assist him with those tasks he was not able to do on his own. She was also blessed to take a free computer class which later equipped her with the necessary skills that landed her next job.

Both families prayed regularly and consistently for God to restore movement to Al's hands, wrists and elbows. Slowly, God did just that! Al can now eat unassisted and enjoy his independence in this area of life again. Praise God!

But that is not the end of their miraculous story. Al and Ever had discussed retirement prior to these events. They had visited Atlanta, Georgia, on several occasions prior to his injuries. Al always said that he would like to retire in Atlanta. When his doctors warned him that the cold in Illinois climate was not good for his condition and that he would not work again, Al and Ever decided it was time for them to move to Atlanta.

Again, prayers from both families continued for about one and a half years. Al waited patiently for the settlement from his job. God moved swiftly as soon as the settlement concluded. During their house hunting trip to Atlanta, they did not find a house easily. Al and Ever looked at several properties, but nothing seemed to match their desires.

Their daughter, Jennifer, advised them to try **one** more sub-division as they prepared to head to the airport en route to Illinois. When Al walked into the kitchen in the house, he felt that his prayer was answered: "Acknowledge God in all thy ways and He will direct one's path," Proverbs 3:6. Both Al and Ever loved the house, so they moved to Atlanta.

They were unsuccessful in selling their home as a "For Sale by Owner". Their daughter, Jennifer, suggested they list the house with a real estate agent, to whom she referred them. The agent listed their house and it sold within two days! They did not even have to come back to Illinois for the closing.

Next, God orchestrated work for Ever in Atlanta. This is where those free computer classes during her lay off, actually paid off. Prior to their relocation to Atlanta, Ever had worked for a national pharmacy chain in its corporate office in Chicago for several years. During her farewell party, one of the top managers joined the festivities and offered to connect her to the management team in Atlanta. This was an unsolicited offer, yet a desire that was requested through prayer. Ever concurred with this plan and praised God for what we now designate as "divine connection!" She started work almost two months after her move to Atlanta.

Six years have passed since God worked out all of these challenges for them. Praise to God for His faithfulness! To God be the glory!

Prayer Jewels:

1) "Trust in the Lord with all thy heart and lean not to thy own understanding. In all thy ways acknowledge Him and He will direct thy paths", Proverbs 3:5-6.

2) "The LORD is my light and my salvation; whom shall I fear? The Lord is the strength of my life; of whom shall I be afraid?

   When the wicked, even mine enemies and my foes, came upon me to eat up my flesh, they stumbled and fell.

3) Though a host should encamp against me, my heart shall not fear: though war should rise against me, in this will I be confident", Psalm 27:1-3.

Sister Florence Johnson is married with two (2) children, one son-in-law and five (5) grandchildren.

In April 1999, my abdomen was filled with fluid. Sister Marilynn called me and asked, "Do you have any excess fluid anywhere in your body?"

I asked her why she inquired. Sister Marilynn told me about her dream with me rolling in my bed in lots of fluid. She asked if I wanted to pray about it. I told her, "Yes, I am at a point for deliverance from this affliction."

Shortly thereafter, I had surgery to remove the fluid. We prayed for surgical success "without any complications". God did just that! I recuperated quickly, thank God!

When I got through this situation, I had to face the other affliction in my back. I needed lumbar disc surgery in September 1999. I was able to walk out of the hospital; but my recovery took several months. It was very hard to sleep, lay, sit or stand.

However, I want to declare that God **"answered prayer"** according to Isaiah 53:4-5. He daily gave me strategies to use to facilitate my healing. I praise Him!

My husband was in the midst of a job transition during this time. It is just like God to have everything work together for good when we most need His blessing and His presence. Praise God that I am whole now and I am free to sing melodies each day. I learned to trust God and the value of praying friends through these ordeals.

Prayer Jewels:

1) "For the weapons of our warfare are not carnal, but mighty through God to the pulling down of strongholds," II Corinthians 10:4.

2) "But they that wait upon the LORD shall renew their strength; they shall mount up with wings as eagles; they shall run, and not be weary; and they shall walk, and not faint," Isaiah 40:31.

3) "Surely he hath borne our griefs, and carried our sorrows: yet we did esteem him stricken, smitten of God. But he was wounded for our transgressions; he was bruised for our iniquities: the

chastisement of our peace was upon him; and with his stripes we are healed, Isaiah 53:4-5.

Sister Gloria Williams is the mother of two children, the grandmother of two and has one son-in-law.

I want to share two (2) testimonies about prayers that Sister Marilynn and I have prayed for God's deliverance:

First Testimony

There is power in prayer. I can remember that my daughter was failing math in high school. Actually, her grade for the second quarter was "F". I remember praying and agreeing with Sister Marilynn concerning her math grade. We prayed that she would receive an A+ and also have **complete** understanding to solve every problem. By the end of the school year, my daughter excelled to an A+ level. Praise the Lord!

Now she is a tutor to several college students in math. At the present time, she is on maternity leave. She told me last week that several of the students she tutors dropped their math class until she returns. ☺

Second Testimony

I was going through some financial issues and was facing an eviction from my two (2) bedroom apartment. I was issued a five day notice. I prayed with Sister Marilynn concerning my housing issue. We prayed that God would give me favor with the realty company. We also prayed Philippians 4:19 which states that "God would supply all of my needs according to his riches in glory by Christ Jesus". All that I know is everything turned around when I talked to the Building Manager. He cancelled the eviction notice and extended the time for rental payment. I did not move out until it was time. The Lord is my **Refuge** and **Fortress;** He is a very **Present Help** in the time of trouble.

Prayer Jewels:

1) But my God shall supply all your need according to his riches in glory by Christ Jesus, Philippians 4:19.

2) "God is our refuge and strength, a very present help in trouble", Psalm 46:1.

Evangelist Shirley Davis is the mother of four (4) and grandmother of 2 (two).

Sister Marilynn and I prayed for my youngest son, Michael, to be able to remain with a child care provider, since he had issues with the Park District programs, formalized day care centers, Head Start and Mrs. Rush.

God sent Laverne Stewart to assist me. Laverne was able to successfully work with Michael before and after school for several years prior to her move to Arizona. He showed His faithfulness again!

Prayer Jewel:

1) "For she said within herself, If I may but touch his garment, I shall be whole," Matthew 9:21.

Sister **Virginia Brown** is married with five (5) children, grandmother of nine (9) and the great-grandmother of three (3).

First Testimony

Sister Marilynn encouraged me and prayed with me to realize my educational goals. I am nearly sixty years old and attending college. I am on the Dean's List with a 3.750 average! Praise God for His Word!

Second Testimony

My second granddaughter has two (2) children; she did not want to properly care for them. So, my husband and I cared for them for about six months in late 2007. Our prayer had been that God would give her a mind and heart to raise her own children, according to Psalms 113:9. This Scripture states that, "He makes the barren woman the happy mother of children". In this case, we prayed for my granddaughter to be **a happy mother** to her children. She is now reunited with her two children is caring for their daily needs.

God added another feature in the answer to this prayer. He sent her a man that agreed to take care of all three of them. The marriage took place during summer 2008. God does miracles!

Third Testimony

My youngest son was caught up in drugs and crack. We prayed for God's deliverance; now, this young man is a minister for God!

Fourth Testimony

My fourth child preferred not to live at home with us. There was discomfort on her side and ours. Now, God has performed relationship repair as only He can do it. We praise Him!

Fifth Testimony

We prayed for weight loss; I lost 88 lbs. I need to renew that prayer for God's assistance.

Prayer Jewels:

1) He blessing of the LORD, it makes rich, and he adds no sorrow with it," Proverbs 10:22.

2) "If my people, which are called by my name, shall humble themselves, and pray, and seek my face, and turn from their wicked ways; then will I hear from heaven, and will forgive their sin, and will heal their land, II Chronicles 7:14.

Testimony

Several years ago, I had been going through a lot of issues during the prior few months. I was feeling that no one loved me nor cared, including God!

I was a new Christian; it seemed that I had problems from all sides:

1) My in-laws were making comments that my husband needed someone to play with…i.e. e., my sister-in-law's soon to be born child.

2) People were making "insensitive, inconsiderate and overbearing" remarks about our childlessness.

3) I told my mom that I might not be here in the near future. Her response was, "I will need to get myself together if you're not here. I don't know why you wouldn't be here."

I thought my mom would have asked me what was wrong, but she did not.

I was just "overwhelmed" with many thoughts about the three (3) points above as well as I thought about the rejection from my husband, my father-in-law and sister-in-law. I kept thinking about how I married early. My husband was not home. I was just mentally tired.

So, I pulled the car into the garage and left it running… I put the door down… I was just mentally tired!

At that moment, Sister Marilynn called me to inquire what I was doing. I was very quiet and I told her that I was all right and located in the garage. I had been out shopping.

She told me that God gave her an "**urgent unction**" to call me at that precise second as she was putting up her groceries on that Saturday evening.

Sister Marilynn said that she wondered "**why**" I came to her mind with such urgency, if everything was fine. I did not tell her what my plan was a few seconds before she called.

After Sister Marilynn called me to pray and encourage me about "whatever" the issue was. She asked for God's blessings upon my family and reminded me that <u>**"God had not forgotten me at all"**</u>. After the prayer, I turned the car off and got out of the car. I went into my house and cried. I tried calling my husband without success.

I'm glad that Sister Marilynn obeyed that **"urgent unction"** without knowing why or inquiring thereafter about *that day*, until I was ready to tell her about one year later. She was **stunned** and replied that an **"urgent unction"** had never occurred before **without a reason.** Sister Marilynn was very glad that she responded as soon as she understood who needed an immediate **"fervent prayer"**!

Prayer Jewels:

1) Listen carefully for God's directions as he "speaks expressly and clearly" according to I Timothy 4:1.

2) "Keep your lives free from the love of money and be content with what you have, because God has said, Never will I leave you; never will I forsake you", Hebrews 13:5.

Anonymous and Blessed Now

There is a saying among the Christian community, "faith can begin where the will of God is known". Often times we do not receive an answer to our prayers because we do not take the time to seek God's will. After seeking God for His will, we must stand and believe.

Our Testimony

Teresse, my youngest sibling, asked for prayer repeatedly as she attended a California Christian College **debt free!** Praise God! God performed different miracles throughout her four (4) years. He taught Teresse how to believe Him to show up through people, scholarships and work opportunities.

Whenever, Teresse was on the brink of not having money in a timely fashion at the start of the semester, God provided a "divine connection" for her to meet "every need according to His riches in glory", Philippians 4:19.

Over the years Sister James and I have experienced many victories by applying these principles:

1) "Trust God, lean not to your understanding, acknowledge Him in **ALL** of your ways, know He will direct your path", (Proverbs 3:5-6).

2) Have people in your life that will believe God with you and that will **PRAY,** Matthew 18:18-20.

Sister James is the type of friend and prayer warrior you want in your life. She will truly touch and agree with you in prayer. Among our friends, she is the matriarch of faith and prayer. Praise God for her life.

Prayer Jewels:

1) "Trust God, lean not to your understanding, acknowledge Him in **ALL** of your ways, know He will direct your path", (Proverbs 3:5-6).

2) "Verily I say unto you, whatsoever ye shall bind on earth shall be bound in heaven: and whatsoever ye shall loose on earth shall be loosed in heaven.

Again I say unto you, that if two of you shall agree on earth as touching any thing that they shall ask, it shall be done for them of my Father which is in heaven.

For where two or three are gathered together in my name, there am I in the midst of them", per Matthew 18:18-20.

Sister Tiffany Baker
Temecula California

Renee McCline is married and the mother of one young adult.

Marilynn and I met in the early 1990's while working for a major consumer products company. We worked out of a location better known as "North Avenue." We were both a part of the Human Resources Team that supported multiple sites: North Avenue, Grand Avenue and the Distribution Center. We did not see each other on a daily basis but we interacted via phone or by email almost daily.

Our friendship blossomed as a result of little Miss Melissa James. She was a small girl, about 8 or 9 years of age. We were at a Company sponsored event that involved writing letters to a Pen Pal. On that day, I became a life-long pen pal to Melissa and gained a life-long friendship with Marilynn and her family.

Over the years, we have watched our kids grow to young adulthood. We have seen them through many birthdays, graduations, school events, church services and holiday gatherings.

Marilynn is not only my friend; she is as close to me as a sister. We can talk about anything with each other. Let me also say, at some of the lowest points in my life, Marilynn has prayed me through. When I have been in doubt, Marilynn has prayed for me and with me.

My family members have come to know Marilynn through me. Some have met her and others have only heard about Marilynn. This acquaintance is a result of my dad's many hospitalizations over the years. At every hospital stay over at Oak Park Hospital (OPH) Marilynn has made numerous visits and have prayed many prayers. When the doctors said that my dad was not going to make it, Marilynn was right there praying us through the doctors' reports.

One intervention with my dad really stands out. This was in 2004 while he was a patient at OPH. The doctor's had prepared us for the worst. My dad has congestive heart failure, chronic diabetes and many other ailments. On this particular occasion, his endocrine doctor had showed up to pronounce him dead based on his vitals. That night my stomach was in knots. I had spoken with Marilynn earlier in the day and had given her the update.

Marilynn said she would stop by the hospital that evening. It was very close to 8 p.m. and visiting hours were just about over. My dad was in ICU (intensive care unit) so they were much stricter about visiting hours. My mom and I had departed my dad's room and had made our way down to the lobby on the 1st floor of the hospital and we met Sister Marilynn. Sister Marilynn was cheerful as always. She grabbed us both by the hands and we all headed back to my dad's room in ICU. Sister Marilynn anointed my dad's head, face, feet and hands with blessed olive oil.

Dad was not doing a lot of responding but he knew that Marilynn was there. Sister Marilynn prayed fervent prayers over my dad. Her praying got the attention of the nurses' station outside his room. It seemed as if they all stopped working momentarily to peep at us. I believed that night that God was in my dad's room. We all departed the hospital at the same time. Throughout the night, I called back to the ICU to check my dad's status with his nurse. The nurse reported each time, "no change."

The next morning, my mom and I left early to spend the day at the hospital. When we got off the elevator on the 5th floor and walked through the double doors of ICU, we could hear my dad giving the nurses a hard time. We knew that God had answered our prayers. My dad had made a miraculous recovery from the night before! The report that morning was…he will be moved to the "step down" unit which is across the hall from ICU. I know that prayer changes things, and I know that Marilynn's prayers were heard the night before in my dad's room. Prayer had changed my dad's outlook that evening. Praise the Lord! While my dad still has many health challenges, God is good. Dad has a set of special angels watching over him. It has been close to four years now since that episode.

Marilynn is well known in my family and has been adopted as an "official" member of the family. Both my mom and dad have commented on how sweet Marilynn is. They have bragged about how wonderful she is and how lucky we are as a family to have someone like Marilynn in our lives. Marilynn has prayed us through many storms. My mom said, "When you need prayer, you want to call on somebody whose prayers reach the heavens." That would be Sister Marilynn Elaine James.

As a direct result of Sister Marilynn's prayer power over my dad's life, other family members have made the following comments about Sister Marilynn:

"We just love her to death".

"She is as sweet as can be".

"She knows how to pray and doesn't mind praying for you".

"She's like someone you've known all your life".

"No issue is too big or too small to take to her for prayer".

"You all are so lucky to have a sister like that in your lives".

"I feel like I know her and we have never met".

"She is an honorary member of our family too".

"Your dad lights up when he sees Marilynn walk in his hospital room".

I thank God everyday for sending me such an excellent friend! Marilynn has been faithful in our friendship and an active prayer warrior in my life. Over the years she has prayed many, many, many, prayers "with" and "for" me and my family members.

Employment Search Prayers

I have often spoken to "Momma Marilynn" about her prophetic abilities in Christ. It is my belief that Marilynn is a prophet based on the timing of answered prayers.

I learned early in life how to pray and wait on God to deliver. But, it is something about getting Marilynn involved in the prayer requests that brings it to fruition.

Most of us have experienced job loss at one point or another in our lives. If we have not been personally impacted by loss of a job, we certainly know of someone either at home or very close to us that did experience this type of loss.

Personally, I have worked for two (2) employers that have announced plant closures. In my case, I have been fortunate enough to have secured another job prior to my release. However, I have experienced the impact of job loss in my household more than five (5) times. All resulted from plant closures. When this has happened it created lots of emotions and fears. By the grace of God, we made it! But, while going through it we did not know how we would make it.

It is something about job loss. When someone I know or I have lost a job, we have all shared a similar experience that people we used to hear from — quit calling. Folks do not want to talk to you if you do not have a job. That was never the case with Marilynn. No matter the situation, I can rest assured that Marilynn and I will converse.

I distinctly remember an occasion when my husband was out of work for an extended period of time and we needed money. He had gone to several interviews and would get the typical response, "we'll get back to you." At that time, getting back to us was not happening soon enough for me. I needed an instant deliverance so I called Marilynn.

Marilynn immediately began to pray with me on the phone. I could feel the reverence from her prayers through the phone. I then put my husband on the phone; Marilynn began to pray with him, too. As I watched, he closed his eyes and listened closely to the praises over the phone. I remembered as he hung up from the call that he said, "Marilynn is something else, she knows she can pray". I asked him what do you believe, do you believe that God will deliver. He responded, "Yes".

That night was an extremely long night. But, I believed that Joy was going to come in the morning. The next day we awoke to a bright sunny day. I woke up feeling real good. Deep down in my spirit, I knew that God was going to deliver our prayer request for my husband to get a job.

My daughter and I left home to go to the grocery store. As soon as we arrived to the store, my cell phone rang. On the caller ID I saw it was my home number. It was my husband calling me to say that he got the call from his new employer that he got the job! We both sang hallelujah praises!!! My husband's first words were, "Marilynn is something else. Her prayers really reach the heavens". God had delivered not only the prayers for a job but he **blessed him** with a **"good job"**.

Marilynn is an angel and our SHERO (she + hero)!

Marilynn has prayed for promotions; I received them. Marilynn has prayed for success in my meetings; they were successful. Marilynn has prayed for God to clear my mind so that my thoughts can be transformed to actions on paper to construct my presentations, and again, God delivered. God has delivered whatever we have prayed for and have believed.

I have called on Marilynn to pray for my friends and family members as well.

My girlfriend had experienced unemployment for a number of months and had experienced several rejections. In response to her desires for employment, I wanted her to have some extra unction along with her prayer request. So, I talked to Marilynn about her needs. I asked Marilynn to pray some special prayers for her. We needed a "Divine Connection and the Divine Hook-Up". Several days had passed and there was no response. Marilynn and my girlfriend connected by telephone and prayed for God's deliverance. The next day or two, I received a call from my girlfriend, she said, "good news...I got the job." We sang hallelujah praises!!!! God had delivered again; he blessed my friend with a job.

I believe and I know that prayer changes things. Approximately eleven months ago, I prayed for God to deliver me from my place of employment. My job was overwhelming. In actuality, there was more job than there was me to do the job. I was working 12 hour days and on call 24 hours a day. Indeed, this was a unique role. If I tried to put a descriptor on the day-to-day task involved with this job, most would find it hard to believe.

But, you would really have to work there to believe it. I thank God for his Divine Purpose in my life. I truly recognized that my season was about to end on this particular assignment. Both Marilynn and I had prayed for God to afford me 6 months off. Yes, yes, yes...God answered my prayer over and above what we prayed for. God delivered right **on time!** He rescued me from high cholesterol, stress and nutritional issues all directly impacted due to job stress.

Jail Release and Intervention Prayers

Prayer worked in another arena for our family. My brother was arrested and on trial for allegations from law enforcement. There were multiple charges against him. My brother stated that several of the charges were untrue. The sad irony to this story is he was arrested on my dad's birthday. At the time of his arrest, we did not know the extent nor the impact of his charges nor were we prepared for what we endured over the next several months.

My parents, Marilynn and I prayed for almost 18 months for favor over my brother's life. We asked God to allow him to be placed in a rehabilitation program that would deliver some long-term results. Ultimately the judge **mandated** this.

We retained a lawyer for his case. There were times when we did not know if the lawyer would show up to court or if he really had our best interest in this case. The lawyer kept us on pins and needles. There was an occasion when the attorney did not show up to court. He alleged he had written down the wrong date for court. I believed it to be "Divine Intervention" that — the particular date was overlooked or delayed. It was not by happen-stance but God had a better plan. <u>**On the morning of the rescheduled court date, all the charges against my brother were dropped!**</u> We had been praying Acts 12: 4-17. We wanted God to deliver him out of jail just as Apostle Peter was delivered.

One of the State's Attorneys whispered to another lawyer that the (alleged) evidence had disappeared from the police evidence vault. God had been a deliverer in the vault room and a lawyer in the court-room that morning. While my brother did not have to serve any extended jail time, he was placed on probation for two years with mandated participation in a drug rehabilitation program. Per my brother's self report, he has not had any further issues with law enforcement. And, we are still praying and asking God for favor over his life as well as asking God to bless him with full-time employment.

Prayer Jewels:

1) Fret not thyself because of evildoers, neither be thou envious against the workers of iniquity. For they shall soon be cut down like the grass, and wither as the green herb. Trust in the Lord, and do good; so shall thou dwell in the land, and verily thou shall be

fed. Delight thyself also in the Lord; and he shall give thee the desires of thine heart. Psalms 37:1-4

2) If ye have faith as a grain of mustard seed, ye shall say unto this mountain, Remove hence to yonder place; and it shall remove; and nothing shall be impossible unto you. Matthew 17:20.

3) [4]"And when he had apprehended him, he put him in prison, and delivered him to four quaternion of soldiers to keep him; intending after Easter to bring him forth to the people.

[5]Peter therefore was kept in prison: but prayer was made without ceasing of the church unto God for him.

[6]And when Herod would have brought him forth, the same night Peter was sleeping between two soldiers, bound with two chains: and the keepers before the door kept the prison.

[7]And, behold, the angel of the Lord came upon him, and a light shined in the prison: and he smote Peter on the side, and raised him up, saying, Arise up quickly. And his chains fell off from his hands.

[8]And the angel said unto him, Gird thyself, and bind on thy sandals. And so he did. And he said unto him, Cast thy garment about thee, and follow me.

[9]And he went out, and followed him; and wist not that it was true which was done by the angel; but thought he saw a vision.

[10]When they were past the first and the second ward, they came unto the Iron Gate that leads unto the city; which opened to them of his own accord: and they went out, and passed on through one street; and forthwith the angel departed from him.

[11]And when Peter was come to himself, he said, now I know of a surety, that the LORD hath sent his angel, and hath delivered me out of the hand of Herod, and from all the expectation of the people of the Jews.

[12]And when he had considered the thing, he came to the house of Mary the mother of John, whose surname was Mark; where many were gathered together praying.

[13]And as Peter knocked at the door of the gate, a damsel came to hearken, named Rhoda.

[14]And when she knew Peter's voice, she opened not the gate for gladness, but ran in, and told how Peter stood before the gate.

[15]And they said unto her, Thou art mad. But she constantly affirmed that it was even so. Then said they, It is his angel.

[16]But Peter continued knocking: and when they had opened the door, and saw him, they were astonished.

[17]But he, beckoning unto them with the hand to hold their peace, declared unto them how the Lord had brought him out of the prison. And he said; Go show these things unto James, and to the brethren. And he departed, and went into another place," Acts 12:4-17.

Sister Margo Porsche is married and has eight (8) children along with twelve (12) grandchildren.

In early 2003, **Sister Margo** connected with this author during Corporate Prayer at Living Word Christian Center. Sister Margo had a long term request to receive her high school diploma.

Margo and this author prayed for approximately five (5) years for manifestation of this request. Margo attended many programs in an attempt to complete this dream. She studied with the author one-on-one from the G.E.D. (General Education) manual on three (3) separate occasions. Also, Margo attended formal study sessions with Living Word

Christian Center and other community-based programs. None of these avenues got her to the high school diploma finish line.

God provided a fifteen (15) week community-based school program during the fall of 2007 in Chicago. Margo attended night school and finally reached her dream from her youth! Yes, His faithfulness extends to any unfulfilled desire! Praise God for His ability to perform miracles and "divine connections"!

Prayer Jewels:

1) "His mercies are new every morning: great is His faithfulness", Lamentations 3:23.

2) "Wisdom is the principal thing; therefore, get wisdom: and with all thy getting get understanding", Proverbs 4:7.

Sister Tanya Briggs is a prayer warrior for many Christians at her church and in her family.

Testimony One

Uncle Roscoe was in a severe accident on February 15, 2008. Read the email/newspaper summary below:

From: Tanya Briggs

To: Marilynn James

The Press Democrat has a story today:

"Clearlake. Woman killed in Highway 29 crash.

"A 76 year-old Clearlake woman was killed Friday and another driver seriously injured in a head-on collision that closed Highway 29 in Lake County for more than an hour.

"The woman's name was not released pending notification of her family...Authorities also withheld the name of the 85 year old Clearlake Oaks man who suffered major injuries in the 9:50 am crash, saying his family hadn't been contacted.

"The collision occurred just north of Hofacker Lane between Lower Lake and Hidden Valley. The woman, driving southbound, drifted into northbound traffic for unknown reasons, the CHP said.

"Her 2004 Ford Focus collided with the 2005 Chevrolet Impala driven by the Clearlake Oaks man, the CHP said. "The incident closed Highway 29 for nearly 90 minutes. The injured man was taken by air ambulance to Santa Rosa Memorial Hospital. His condition was not known."

****

February 19, 2008

Forwarded message to: Marilynn James

Subject: Roscoe

To: Tanya Briggs

Hi!

Good news. We have just returned from visiting Roscoe at the hospital in Santa Rosa. He is progressing to the point where he will be transferred to Kaiser Hospital in San Francisco today.

Roscoe is quite banged up but is alert and knows what's being said and tries to respond.

He is a living example of the power of prayer. Thank you.

Frankie

****

March 6, 2008

From: Tanya Briggs

To: Marilynn James

Remember, we started with my 85 year old Uncle Roscoe in critical condition from a head-on collision on Friday, February 15th. He started out in critical condition with many broken bones. The driver that hit him was **killed instantly.**

We prayed for a speedy recovery with no complications and no long-term effects to his motor skills, etc.

The doctors and nurses call him a "Miracle Man" and he is fast on the road to recovery, memory included, without complications. He is expected to make a full recovery. Hallelujah!! To God be the Glory!

****

Thu, 8 May 2008 13:03:33-0500

From: Tanya Briggs

To: Marilynn James

Uncle Roscoe is doing well and has moved into his Assisted Living apartment. He is grateful to God and knows that he is God's miracle and gives Him all of the glory for his outcome. Uncle Roscoe is very appreciative of all of the prayers and gets very emotional when speaking about the ordeal.

****

Testimony Two

In 2005, my company announced that there would be no bonuses for any employees, including Sales/Marketing personnel. I was really concerned about this point, since I had already met several of my goals.

I called Sister Marilynn to pray that I would receive what was promised to me. We did touch and agree that God's great faithfulness would be manifested to me. I did receive a bonus for that year!

God did what I asked! I was the only person to receive a bonus for that year!

Testimony Three

During 2006, I was placed on a performance improvement plan (PIP) through a lot of false reports about my work from co-workers and unsubstantiated estimates regarding my sales performance year to date. This was very hurtful and demeaning to me, since I pride myself on doing exceptional work.

My boss chose to believe my co-workers' renditions of truth and had not accurately verified my sales numbers. This meant that I would not be bonus eligible **and** my job was in jeopardy.

Again, Sister Marilynn and I prayed for God's deliverance and vindication. God showed His awesome power! No only was the PIP rescinded resulting in my total vindication, I exceeded plan! I was the **only** person in my Sales/Marketing group to exceed plan for that year!

When God does His work; He does it well. Praise him from whom all blessings flow.

Prayer Jewel:

1) "He suffered no man to do them wrong: yea, he reproved kings for their sakes;

   Saying, Touch not mine anointed, and do my prophets no harm," Psalm 115:14-15.

Sister Joyce Williams is married and has two children.

Testimony One

My aunt is a restaurant owner who had catering books for events at her establishment. As we were conversing one day, she mentioned that the books had mysteriously disappeared after family members visited her.

I called Sister Marilynn so we could pray about the immediate return of her property. We asked God to bring the books back immediately and without confusion.

About a week later, the books arrived mysteriously in the U.S. mail. She was exuberant! No one ever claimed participation in this disappearance.

Testimony Two

I originally worked for CNA Insurance until I was part of the sale to Cunningham Lindsey. Part of the agreement with Cunningham

Lindsey — was that employees of CNA could **not** re-apply to CNA for three (3) years.

I worked for Cunningham Lindsey for less than one year, when we received another announcement of a sale to Broadspire Insurance (this made the original "no re-hire" clause null and void with the Broadspire sale). I was contemplating taking advantage of the severance and finding other employment elsewhere, but not sure what I wanted to do.

As I was thinking about my "next steps" an old friend from CNA called to see how I was doing. I told her of the new sale and she alerted me that there was a job at CNA which met my qualifications. I sent my resume and was called for an interview within a week. By that time, I had decided to accept the severance package. I called Sister Marilynn the morning of the interview to touch and agree in prayer. She prayed, "Dear God, please bless Sister Joyce in the interview. Let her find favor and please give her an immediate response today, by the close of business, in Jesus' name".

Around 4 p.m. on the same day, I received a call from the recruiter. She advised me that "it was highly unusual for the team to make such a quick decision, but they wanted to offer me the job right away". I was able to leave my old company with my severance package intact and begin employment within two (2) weeks. I could not have accomplished this if I tried to plan it myself.

I was so grateful to God for a "quick" answer!" I had His favor and direction. I gave my notice and moved back to CNA. The sale had worked in my favor! Praise God!

Sister Marilynn and I have known each other for more than 10 years and have had the opportunity to touch and agree on a lot of things, and every thing has come to pass. What an amazing person in Christ.

Prayer Jewels:

1) "Behold, how good and how pleasant it is for brethren to dwell together in unity! Psalm 133:1.

2) "No weapon that is formed against thee shall prosper; and every tongue that shall rise against thee in judgment thou shall condemn, Isaiah 54:17.

3) [1]I will bless the LORD at all times: his praise shall continually be in my mouth.

[2]My soul shall make her boast in the LORD: the humble shall hear thereof, and be glad.

[3]O magnify the LORD with me, and let us exalt his name together.

[4]I sought the LORD, and he heard me, and delivered me from all my fears.

[5]They looked unto him, and were lightened: and their faces were not ashamed.

[6]This poor man cried, and the LORD heard him, and saved him out of all his troubles.

[7]The angel of the LORD encamped round about them that fear him, and delivered them.

[8]O taste and see that the LORD is good: blessed is the man that trusted in him.

[9]O fear the LORD, ye his saints: for there is no want to them that fear him.

[10]The young lions do lack, and suffer hunger: but they that seek the LORD shall not want any good thing.

[11]Come, ye children, hearken unto me: I will teach you the fear of the LORD.

[12]What man is he that desired life, and loved many days, that he may see good?

[13]Keep thy tongue from evil and thy lips from speaking guile.

[14]Depart from evil, and do good; seek peace, and pursue it.

[15]The eyes of the LORD are upon the righteous, and his ears are open unto their cry.

[16]The face of the LORD is against them that do evil, to cut off the remembrance of them from the earth.

[17]The righteous cry and the LORD hears, and delivered them out of all their troubles.

[18]The LORD is nigh unto them that are of a broken heart; and saved such as be of a contrite spirit.

[19]Many are the afflictions of the righteous: but the LORD delivered him out of them all.

[20]He kept all his bones: not one of them is broken.

[21]Evil shall slay the wicked: and they that hate the righteous shall be [22]The LORD redeemed the soul of his servants: and none of them that trust in him shall be desolate, Psalm 34.

Sister Atalaya (Atty) Kenyatta is a sister who regularly prays for her family to know the Lord.

I have a car that I purchased from my sister; however, I do not have a driver's license yet. This meant that my car remained parked in the private parking space on my condo lot.

In 2006, the Village Police came onto the private parking lot and issued me several tickets regarding my license plate sticker and the fact that the car was not being moved each day. Since the car was stationary, the car appeared "inoperable" to the Police. The tickets written totaled approximately $1700. I was surprised that the Police came onto private property to issue tickets, so I went to the Village Police Station.

Other citizens were there; so I bought the license plate sticker. The Lord directed me to leave. I decided to await further instructions from the Lord.

I returned home and called Sister Marilynn to pray for the "next steps". We prayed for God's favor to cancel the tickets; since I had not driven the car, just parked it. We scripted out a letter for me to send to the Village.

When I called the Village Police to follow-up on the receipt of the letter, favor poured into my life. The Village Clerk answered and advised me to: "hold on, while she spoke with another employee".

The Village Clerk returned to the phone and advised me, "The Law Enforcement made a mistake. All of the tickets are cancelled". Sister Marilynn and I praised God for canceling the tickets through prayer and follow-up! I said, "<u>We only needed to speak God's word only!</u>

Testimony Two

My mom is a pre-kindergarten and kindergarten teacher and my mom has been dedicated to the Muslim belief structure; therefore, she would not hear anything about Christianity.

As Sister Marilynn and I have prayed diligently for my family, my mom now asks for Scriptures. My mom quickly writes the references and verses as well as listens to Pastors Joel Osteen, T. D. Jakes and Bill Winston. Praise God for miracles in the soul!

Testimony Three

My sister, (VAS), told me recently that I was a blessing to her. VAS advised her friend that I had been very faithful to her. I blessed her and her children while she has been in the armed services.

VAS wrote a letter outlining how one needs favor on one's life, what it means to be blessed and gave recognition that her estate would have been diminished without my assistance.

This was very touching to me, since my sister oftentimes declined to hear the Word of God. God has a way of proving His faithfulness.

Testimony Four

I have been promoted several times in the past few years as a direct result of the prayers for promotion, Psalm 75:6:

"For promotion cometh neither from the east, nor from the west, nor from the south".

Subsequently, prayer was needed to obtain the proper training in the new positions and proper introductions to clients that were assigned to me. As we have prayed for God's glory to manifest in these situations with overwork and/or overwhelm feelings, God lifted the burdens with each prayer. These were times for spiritual warfare, since I was under attack. How great is His faithfulness!

Prayer Jewels:

1) "The centurion answered and said, Lord, I am not worthy that thou shouldest come under my roof: but speak the word only, and my servant shall be healed.

For I am a man under authority, having soldiers under me: and I say to this man, Go, and he goes; and to another, Come, and he cometh; and to my servant, Do this, and he doeth it.

When Jesus heard it, he marveled, and said to them that followed, Verily I say unto you, I have not found so great faith, no, not in Israel", St. Matthew 8: 8-10.

2) "And they overcame him by the blood of the Lamb, and by the word of their testimony; and they loved not their lives unto the death", Revelation 12:11.

3) "Now thanks be unto God, which always causes us to **triumph** in Christ, and makes manifest the savor of his knowledge by us in every place," II Corinthians 2:14.

Sister Sheryl Thomas is married and has two (2) children.

Sister Marilynn encouraged me to get my foster care license repeatedly over several months, since my husband and I planned to be foster parents. We delayed because our work schedules were not similarly aligned.

As soon as we made the steps to go to the foster care and educational advocacy classes, everything immediately worked in harmony! My husband was able to get permission to leave work during the day shift. My clients were amenable to my changing their hair salon appointments. The agency helped us get classes together on the same days.

What I learned in this experience is that <u>we have to take steps</u> to have our dreams manifest. The ironic thing is that the oldest boy looks exactly like my husband and the youngest boy looks like me.

When confusion surfaced about the license specifics as we were being offered children under one (1) year old, the foster care counselor was on hand to verify that we had taken all of the coursework required for those under one. Praise God! <u>I learned what it meant to have others continually praying for a new undertaking.</u>

When the agency determined to return the oldest boy to his grandparents in Tennessee, we prayed for God to reverse this desire, since he had been with us for years. The grandparents' rights were ultimately revoked. Sister James kept advising me that God grants our petitions according to Philippians 4:6.

There is power in agreement. All things truly work together for good to those of us who love the Lord. I praise God for Sister James' friendship and continuous prayers for my family.

Prayer Jewels:

1) "Do not be anxious about anything, but in everything, by prayer and petition, with thanksgiving, present your requests to God," Philippians 4:6.

2) For the vision is yet for an appointed time, but at the end it shall speak, and not lie: though it tarry, wait for it; because it will surely come, it will not tarry", Habakkuk 2:3 .

This version of the testimony was written in <u>April 2008</u> as God unfolded His complete deliverance for Sister Sheryl. Read on and know God gives complete answers to prayer.

Sister Sheryl Thomas is married and has two children.

Where do I begin? I will take note from the book of Psalms and begin with thanksgiving and praise. I thank God for choosing me and empowering me with all that I need to prosper. I thank Him for His thoughts being higher than my thoughts. I praise God for the plan that He has for my life.

I thank God for my husband, children and family. I praise Him for deliverance, healing, strength, prosperity and a sound mind. I am **"fully persuaded"** that the good work He started in me will come to completion and fruition.

I am 38 years old. I grew up in a façade of a loving, suburban home which behind closed doors was chaotic and abusive. There was physical, mental and drug abuse. Also, woven into these issues was infidelity and adultery.

The bible says, "train up a child in the way that s (he) should go. And when (s) he is older (s) he will not depart from it", Proverbs 22:6. Depending upon the life that one is living…this point can be a blessing or a curse the children in the family. Since God called heaven and earth to record against the Israelites their worship of other gods, **God wants us to choose life so that both our generation and our children may live to the fullest,** Deuteronomy, 30: 17-19.

Here we go!

By 17 years old I had:

- Used alcohol

- Tried marijuana

- Stolen marijuana from my parents to give to other teens, so they would let me hang with them

- Had my first sexual experience with a 24 year old so-called male and

- Lost every sense of innocence and self-esteem.

All of this confusion and dysfunction ended in a broken heart, loss of trust and a trip to Charter Barkley (a mental institution for teens). My spirit was so broken that I began to cry without the ability to stop.

My parents were entangled with their issues and they believed that I was suicidal. I stayed for almost two (2) weeks as I remember back to the time. I had intense therapy with my doctors so that I was able to express my issues to my parents. We all agreed to do better. I was discharged. My parents kept a watchful eye for a minute, but we all fell short.

My next phase was the road to promiscuity. Then, I desired to be desirable no matter the cost. I did not know at the time that sexual intercourse opens one to having a soul tie in the spiritual realm. This sexual deposit has no return spiritual value, (no deposit and no return).

I began to date nice guys, not-so nice guys, cute guys, and "bad guys". I even dated a drug dealer. I did date some of them at the same time. I did not know the Scripture at the time that the "thief comes not, but to steal, and to kill and to destroy, Jesus came that they might have life, and have it more abundantly," John 10:10.

The devil was trying to set me up to kill me. The choices that I was making seemed to be in agreement with the devil's plan.

The last guy that I dated before change would come was shot at point blank range in the head while a young lady was sitting next to him in his car. Our relationship had dwindled and I thought it was me who lost my desire for him. I now know that the "steps of a Good Man are ordered by the Lord", Psalm 37:23. The Lord did not order me to be with him at that time. So, God delivered me and took away the desire. Praise God for intercessors!

In my process of "losing" my desire for man who was shot, (R.I. P. — R. S. G.), I met a nice young man while I was out with my girlfriends.

At first, I did not like him since he worked a 9-5 job. He was not a flashy dresser nor did he drive fancy cars.

"But the LORD said unto Samuel, Look not on his countenance, or on the height of his stature; because I have refused him: for the LORD sees not as man sees; for man looks on the outward **appearance,** but the LORD looks on the heart," I Samuel 16:7.

This man began to show great concern for my well-being. He drove me to work, brought lunches, picked me up from work and just spent genuine time with me. This was unusual and peculiar to me.

To understand the magnitude of his gestures, I must add that I was self-employed and made cash daily. I got off work around 9 p.m. or there-after; I would take the Chicago Transit Authority (C.T.A.) buses and trains to the Medical Center stop. There, all manner of people hung out. It was a rough area!

Since he assured that I got home safely, I felt that he was my blessing in disguise. Thank God for angels!

Eleven and a half months after we started dating; we married. I was 23 years old. Guess what kind of marriage we began to have...

We both grew up in dysfunction, so that is what we brought to the table. It was a mess, but I think that someone was praying in tongues. Those prayers in conjunction with Jesus' prayers saved us.

I began to attend Living Word Christian Center (LWCC) after hearing that one of the girls that was a known "hell raiser" attended this church. I knew that her life was changed!

I sneaked to the 7 a.m. service and then I would go to my traditional church at 11 a.m.

My mom went to the traditional church for years; she was an usher.

Living Word taught me the Word regarding:

- Healing
- Deliverance

- Receiving the Holy Ghost (Holy Spirit)

- Generational curses

- Binding and loosing through prayer

- Faith and a multitude of other gifts and

- Making confessions in accordance with the Word of God for anything that I desired

The music was different but the Word was alive and "kicking"! My favorite Scripture is:

"As it is written, I have made thee a father of many nations, before him whom he (Abraham) believed, even God, who quickens the dead, and calls those things which be not as though they were," Romans 4:17.

The Word that Pastor William Winston taught made me free indeed, according to John 8:32. Ultimately, I left the old church. As my mom saw that "fruit" of my life was good, she left, too! Eventually, my husband came to LWCC also!

Everything seemed perfect now — but not quite!

We had been married for years and now we wanted children. I read every scripture I could find regarding redemption regarding sickness (barrenness). I spoke diligently to my body to line-up and bring forth a child. I used James 1:2-8 as my prayer and confession base. Still no babies!

James 1:2-8:

"2My brethren, count it all joy when ye fall into divers temptations;

3Knowing this, that the trying of your faith works patience.

4But let patience have her perfect work, that ye may be perfect and entire, wanting nothing.

[5]If any of you lack wisdom, let him ask of God, that gives to all men liberally, and upbraids not; and it shall be given him.

[6]But let him ask in faith, nothing wavering. For he that wavers is like a wave of the sea driven with the wind and tossed.

[7]For let not that man think that he shall receive any thing of the Lord.

[8]A double minded man is unstable in all his ways.

In our quest to help God, we played Sarah and Abraham, [meaning we assisted God in supplying a child for us]. My client had a niece named Tatianna. We fell in love with her at first sight. She was almost four (4) months old.

Her mom had died and the father was not in the picture. My client had four (4) biological children and was unable to raise another child. So, we did!

We nurtured her as if she was out seed and had grown in my womb. It was a wonderful feeling/experience, but it was built on confusion. **We know now** that "God **is not** the **author** of **confusion,** but of peace, I Corinthians 14:33a. **God is the author of our faith.**

After 19 months of nurturing, dealing with the woes of teething, observing her first steps and celebrating her first birthday…Tatianna was gone.

After Tatianna left, my husband spent more time away from home. Her departure left me feeling empty and rejected. Relatives taunted me about our childless state. My feelings sank low as I felt that I was not a complete woman. At this point in my life, "low" was a very optimistic word for my state of mind.

In the midst of this confusion, I met Mama Marilynn. He is an on-time God! She sat in my salon chair because another hair stylist could not take her for the set appointment that day; and I had an available appointment. This one appointment has grown into years of friendship. God set-up a **"divine appointment"** for both of us.

Mama Marilynn has taught me to:

- Pray

- Stand and pray again

- Pray for the doors to my salon to be replaced by the building owner who vowed that he would **not** do so

- Give cheerfully

- Pray and believe that mountains in my life would be moved with "my" faith and

- Keep my voice "slow and low" while discussing difficult issues with others.

Mama Marilynn kept reinforcing the truths about:

- The Love of God

- How much God loves me and

- Not being alarmed with every adverse situation; I needed to know that these episodes were "simply tests".

Sister Marilynn began to encourage us to get our foster parenting license. In my young Christian days, I knew that her statement was out-of-the-box. I believed that none would be barren. My children h-a-d to come from my body.

She persisted and kept encouraging us until we got our license. We had favor of God with our licensing agent and our jobs. Everything meshed! We were ready for a baby.

I began to sow in every area that I had a need. I wanted children; so I helped people with their children. I wanted a home; so I helped women with children keep their homes in order.

One Christmas, we had been through hard times. We were unable to purchase gifts due to a slump in our circumstances. Yes, I was saved, but still human. I decided to help a friend wrap her children's gifts.

While away, the agency called with a newborn. I was sowing seed and my husband was working. The answering machine got the message.

I was frantic! I rushed to call to advise the agency to bring us our gift! I learned that the child had been placed with another family, since I was not available at the time of the call. The enemy taunted me in my mind so fervently, telling me that I had missed out and was made a fool.

In retrospect, I see that "God is not mocked, whatever a man sows that shall he reap", Galatians 6:7.

The episode of missing the child landed me in my running car with the garage door down. I heard the enemy say, "Give up, nothing works for you." The devil was a liar! After thinking that everyone had rejected me — even God, my cell phone rang.

It was Mama Marilynn. She inquired regarding my whereabouts and activities. I calmly responded with a generic answer, but she began to warfare in prayer for me as well as spoke life into my spirit. She prayed a prayer that only the "Secret Squirrel" in my conscience or the Holy One could know the depth of prayer that I needed that day, at that moment. We ended the call; I went into my house and began weeping and repenting. I thanked God that He <u>did</u> care and He <u>had not forgotten</u> about me!

I never shared this with my husband or Mama Marilynn until approximately a year later. When I shared it with Mama Marilynn, she recalled the urgency that God yelled in her spirit to contact me ASAP (as soon as possible).

Thereafter, I ate more word, wrote more confessions for deposit in my spirit and 4 (four) months later — we got THE CALL!

When I went to pick up our son, he was turning the agency out with his continual crying.

I picked him up and I began to talk to him; he instantly quieted down. People in the agency came to see if he was okay, since he was so quiet. This was our baby.

My encouragement to anyone in this predicament is to read the following Scripture,

"For the **vision** is yet for an appointed time, but at the end it shall speak, and not lie: **though** it **tarry**, **wait for it;** because it will surely come, it will not **tarry**", Habakkuk 2:3.

The prayer will come true. Wait for it!

He looked so much like my husband; it was miraculous. People who knew his origin commented about his distinct features that were so similar to his father's. Others who did not know his origin commented, "You did not have anything to do with him. He is just like his father". Yes, my son is just like his father, Abba Father!

It was harvest time. The Word that I had confessed became flesh and materialized in our lives!

Months after receiving our bundle of joy, the agency informed us that he would not be staying since the biological, maternal grandparents wanted him in Tennessee. The agency worker spoke this point to me. I heard her and **never** came into verbal agreement that he was leaving.

She **thought** that I was crazy. However, I knew that God uses the foolish things of the world to confound the wise (the ones in charge), I Corinthians 1:27a. I simply did not agree with her **verbally** that he was leaving.

The grandparents received the interstate compact approval to transport our <u>son.</u> We were supposed to send him. Department of Children and Family Services (DCFS) said, "Yes, send him". God said, "No".

At the last minute, something happened in the grandparents' home to cause their approval to be revoked. He was to stay with us!

The birth mother worked to receive parental rights again. However, in the end, she voluntarily relinquished her rights. Glory to God!

We did foster parent another boy, Bobby. He did not stay. It was difficult when he left, because we loved our children intensely.

We never have treated them as DCFS (Department of Children and Family Service) children or wards of the State of Illinois. Those prayer warriors in our inner circle prayed fervently for our well-being.

Two (2) days later, baby # 2 came. He was sixteen (16) days old. He was so beautiful and from the first moment, I knew that he was ours. The second young man favors me. He has my complexion and beautiful, curly, black hair.

Once again, the Lord gave me beauty for ashes:

"To appoint unto them that mourn in Zion, to give unto them **beauty** for **ashes,** the oil of joy for mourning, the garment of praise for the spirit of heaviness; that they might be called trees of righteousness, the planting of the LORD, that he might be glorified," Isaiah 61:3.

By this time, our oldest son was about fifteen (15) months old and we had a new baby. Our children are like olives plants around our table and as arrows in the hand of the mighty.

"Thy wife shall be as a fruitful vine by the sides of thy house: thy children like **olive plants** round about thy table, Psalm 128:3.

During August 2007, one adoption was completed for one of our sons; we awaiting the completion of the second adoption any day. Subsequently, my husband and I celebrated fifteen (15) years of marriage February 2008.

Through all of my circumstances God has proven that Jesus is the same and faithful—yesterday, today and forever, Hebrews 13:8. I cannot tell you why this happened to me, but I thank God for victory through it all.

If God did not love me and my choices were counted in my fate, I would be lost and dead! I praise God for Jesus' obedience, since He took all of my sin to the cross and paid my debts!

If Mama Marilynn had not prayed, I could have been in hell due to my planned suicide which is unpardoned sin. I would not have known what God had in store for me in the future.

"But as it is written, **Eye** hath **not seen,** nor ear heard, neither have entered into the heart of man, the things which God hath prepared for them that love him, 1 Corinthians 2:9.

Summarizing these events has humbled me, healed me and released me. Writing for this project has made me fall deeper in love with God and those that He has appointed to my life, especially my husband, children and family.

I know that God has more for us! He has promised that after the trials we would give Him glory!

"That the **trial** of **your faith,** being much more precious than of gold that perishes, though it be tried with fire, might be found unto praise and honor and glory at the appearing of Jesus Christ:", I Peter 1:7.

Mama Marilynn has assisted me in being **"fully persuaded"** regarding God's power.

"For I am convinced that neither death nor life, neither angels nor demons, neither the present nor the future, nor any powers, neither height nor depth, nor anything else in all creation, will be able to separate us from the love of God that is in Christ Jesus our Lord," Romans 8:38-39.

Thank you, Jesus and Mama Marilynn for allowing me to share these events. **I pray that someone reading this segment will be touched, healed, delivered or given a spark of hope <u>to trust God.</u> I don't care what it looks like. Keep faith like a mustard seed.**

"It is like a mustard seed, which is the smallest seed you plant in the ground. Yet when planted, it grows and becomes the largest of all garden plants, with such big branches that the birds of the air can perch in its shade," Mark 4:31-32.

Know that I relinquished my hair salon when the children came; however, their adoptions are nearly complete now. God has restored my ownership of the same salon! Pastor William (Bill) Winston taught me to make confessions with the Word of God. All of my circumstances now follow the confessions that I made repeatedly. Thank you, Pastor Bill Winston for giving us the truth. Truth is indeed life changing!

Love,
"Sista" Sheryl

Note: (Sheryl was empowered by God to fully relate her testimonies for another's deliverance in May 2008. God told me to wait on her final segment before printing the book).

Prayer Jewels:

1) "It is like a mustard seed, which is the smallest seed you plant in the ground. Yet when planted, it grows and becomes the largest of all garden plants, with such big branches that the birds of the air can perch in its shade," Mark 4:31-32.

2) "For I am convinced that neither death nor life, neither angels nor demons, neither the present nor the future, nor any powers, [39]neither height nor depth, nor anything else in all creation, will be able to separate us from the love of God that is in Christ Jesus our Lord," Romans 8:38-39.

3) "That the **trial** of **your faith,** being much more precious than of gold that perishes, though it be tried with fire, might be found unto praise and honor and glory at the appearing of Jesus Christ:", I Peter 1:7.

4) "Thy wife shall be as a fruitful vine by the sides of thy house: thy children like **olive plants** round about thy table, Psalm 128:3.

5) "To appoint unto them that mourn in Zion, to give unto them **beauty** for **ashes,** the oil of joy for mourning, the garment of praise for the spirit of heaviness; that they might be called trees of righteousness, the planting of the LORD, that he might be glorified," Isaiah 61:3.

6) "But God hath chosen the foolish things of the world to confound the wise; and God hath chosen the weak things of the world to confound the things which are mighty", I Corinthians 1:27.

7) "For the **vision** is yet for an appointed time, but at the end it shall speak, and not lie: **though** it **tarry, wait for it;** because it will surely come, it will not **tarry**", Habakkuk 2:3.

8) "Be not deceived; God is not mocked: for whatsoever a man sows, that shall he also reap", Galatians 6:7.

9) "As it is written, I have made thee a father of many nations, before him whom he (Abraham) believed, even God, who quickens the dead, and calls those things which be not as though they were," Romans 4:17.

10) "After Job had prayed for his friends, the LORD made him prosperous again and gave him **twice** as much as he had before," Job 42:10.

ABOUT THE AUTHOR

Marilynn James has been married to Darnell James for over twenty-three years and she is the mother to Dwight (21) and Melissa (19). They reside in a suburb of Chicago, IL.

Marilynn continues to teach Spanish with the Adult Education Ministry at Living Word Christian Center in Forest Park, IL. She also serves in the Corporate Prayer and Pastoral Care Ministries.

Marilynn plans to start a prayer ministry where individuals can present their prayer requests to an in-person prayer minister, by God's grace and help, in the future.

Marilynn is presently the Clinical Nurse Supervisor for a major third party insurance administrator in Hoffman Estates, IL.